The Day-Spring

The Day-Spring

The Story of the Unknown Apostle to the Americas

Orlo Miller

Hanson

McClelland and Stewart Limited

ISBN: 0-7710-5864-0

The Canadian Publishers
McClelland and Stewart Limited
25 Hollinger Road, Toronto

PHOTO CREDITS

The American Museum of Natural History: **pp. i, ii (bottom)**
Ferdinand Anton: **p. vi (right)**
J. L. Eder, Windsor, Ont. collection: **pp. xii (top left and right), xiii**
Campbell Grant (drawing): from H. S. Gladwin, *Men Out of Asia* McGraw-Hill,
   New York: **p. ii (top left)**
Hankins Collection, Mexico City: **p. iv (top)**
Maridon Miller: **p. xv (top)**
Musée de l'Homme, Paris: **jacket photo and p. iv (bottom)**
Museo nacional de antropologia, Mexico City: **pp. iii, v, vii, xii (bottom)**
Douglas Paisley, Sarnia, Ont. (photograph); from the author's collection:
   pp. ix (bottom), xvi
Pemex Travel Club Bulletin, Mexico City, Sept. 1, 1956: **p. ii (top right)**
Constantino Reyes-Valerio (photograph); from Irene Nicholson, *Mexican and
   Central American Mythology*, Paul Hamlyn, London: **pp. vi, xi (bottom)**
Josué Saenz Collection, Mexico City: **p. ix (top left)**
Smithsonian Institution, Washington, D.C.: **p. xiv (bottom)**
Staatliche Museen, Berlin: **p. ix (top right)**
Alfred Stendahl (photograph); from the Dallas Museum of Art: **p. viii (right)**
Henri Stierlin: **p. xv (bottom)**
Señora de Villafranca collection, Mexico City: **p. x**
From Alexander von Wuthenau, *Pre-Columbian Terracottas*, Methuen, London:
   pp. viii (left), xi (top)

Every reasonable effort has been made to ascertain ownership of the illustrations
used. Information would be welcomed that would enable the publisher to rectify
any error.

Contents

For Maridon

And thou, child, shalt be called the prophet of the Highest: for thou shalt go before the face of the Lord to prepare his ways;

To give knowledge of salvation unto his people for the remission of their sins;

Through the tender mercy of our God; whereby the day-spring from on high hath visited us;

To give light to them that sit in darkness, and in the shadow of death, to guide our feet into the way of peace.

The Gospel According to St. Luke
Chapter One, Verses 76 through 79.

Acknowledgements

I wish to acknowledge with gratitude some of the many people whose encouragement, advice, and assistance over a period of many years have made this book possible.

My thanks are due to the late Right Reverend Dr. George N. Luxton, sixth Bishop of the Anglican Diocese of Huron, Canada; to the late Murray Shapinsky and to Mrs. Irene Shapinsky, of Mexico City, and to my wife, Maridon, for their unfailing understanding and encouragement.

To Dr. Ignacio Bernal, director of the National Museum of Anthropology of Mexico; the Reverend Dr. G.H. Parke-Taylor, dean of theology at Huron College, London, Ontario, and to Mr. Joseph L. Eder, of Windsor, Ontario, my thanks for special assistance in my research.

I want to express my thanks also to Dr. James J. Talman, formerly chief librarian of the University of Western Ontario, London, Canada; the staff of the London Public Library, especially Miss Elizabeth Spicer, of the Reference Department; the staff of the Rancho La Puerta, Tecate, Baja California, Mexico; Señor Arturo Diaz, of Merida, Mexico, and Mr. David Strye, of Cuernavaca, Mexico, for much help and encouragement.

My special thanks to Mr. Geoffrey Ashe, of England, and to Dr. Cyrus H. Gordon, chairman of the Department of Mediterranean Studies of Brandeis University, for reading the manuscript and making many useful suggestions and comments.

Finally, my thanks are due to my typist, Mrs. J. A. Sussex.

To all these and to Mexico itself, my second mother, my affectionate thanks.

Introduction

The Spanish conquerors of Mexico and Peru – Hernando Cortés and Francisco Pizarro – had their task made infinitely easier for them by the existence of a legend that was in the sixteenth century already more than a thousand years old. The Aztec empire delayed, fatally, in mounting its resistance to the troops of Hernando Cortés, believing him to be Quetzalcoatl, a white, bearded culture-hero who had visited Mexico centuries before, promising to return one day. The troops of the powerful Inca kingdom also faltered in superstitious awe before the white soldiers of Francisco Pizarro, believing the leader of that expedition to be the returning Viracocha, who also was white of skin and bearded. He, too, far back in the reaches of legend, had promised to return.

The *conquistadores* and their companions, the Spanish friars, found similar legends throughout their new dominions. The name of the culture-hero differed according to the region and the languages spoken by the people, but his essential features were everywhere the same. Like the Europeans, he was white and bearded, he was a teacher of new ideas, he came from the east and after a number of years he went away, promising to return.

The armies of the Christian Church, like the armies of the Christian states, found the task of conversion made easier by the existence of interesting religious practices accompanying the pervasive legend. In many areas – particularly the Valley of Mexico and the peninsula of Yucatan – they discovered ritual practices which resembled Christian rites. Especially important and significant were the rituals of baptism, confession, and absolution.

There was at first great excitement and enthusiasm among the Spanish priests over these discoveries. Almost immediately there were attempts to identify the mysterious white culture-hero as the far-ranging

11

Apostle, St. Thomas. Closer acquaintance with the native civilizations they had overthrown speedily disillusioned the priesthood. The practices they had initially taken to be Christian-inspired differed in important particulars from the rites endorsed by the Roman Church. Further, the native rites were inextricably involved with other, obviously pagan, practices, including human sacrifice.

By 1542 most of the leading churchmen in the new lands including Fray Diego de Landa, who was later to become first bishop of Yucatan, had decided that all similarities between the native faith and Christianity were perversions, and were the work, not of St. Thomas, but of the devil. In pursuance of his decision de Landa gathered together all the native manuscripts he could find in his jurisdiction and burned them in a great *auto-da-fé* in the village of Mani, Yucatan, on March 16, 1562. It is doubtful whether the Mayan religious library could have solved the mystery of the identity of the American culture-hero, but because of certain unique features of the Yucatecan version of the legend, the burned books might have provided invaluable clues.

It is the thesis of this book that the Mexican legend of Quetzalcoatl – the Feathered Serpent – and its counterparts in other regions of Latin America, conceal the figure of an historical person who crossed the Atlantic in company with others in the first half of the second century of the Christian era, bringing with him many elements of primitive Christianity. It is not my intention to credit to this putative adventurer the origin of the native civilizations of this area. It is now abundantly apparent that the amazing accomplishments of these native societies were largely homegrown products. Their achievements were based upon an agricultural development which in many respects parallels that of the ancient lands of Asia Minor. It *is* my intention, however, to demonstrate the strong probability that this presumed transatlantic contact profoundly influenced the religious beliefs and practices of the high cultures of Mexico, and Central and South America.

The evidence adduced in support of this claim has been marshalled into sections in order to strengthen the argument, to clarify the issues involved for the benefit of future scholars, and to facilitate attack by those with a mind to do so.

This is by no means intended to be a definitive work. Rather it is offered in the hope of encouraging further detailed examination of a legend which was as widespread in the New World as was that of King Arthur in the Old.

Our examination begins with the legend itself.

PART I

THE LEGEND

Chapter One

QUETZALCOATL

He who was perfect in all the customs, exercises and doctrines used by
the ministers of the idols, they elected as high pontiff, whom they called
king or lord, and all the chiefs called him Quetzalcoatl . . . . In the
election no attention was paid to lineage, but only to the customs and
exercises, doctrine and good life . . . he was elected who was virtuous,
humble and peace-loving, and considerate and prudent, and not friv-
olous but grave and austere . . . and loving and merciful and compas-
sionate and a friend of all, and devout, and fearful of god.

— Fr. Bernardino de Sahagún, *Historia general.*

1

On Good Friday, April 22, 1519, two great religious traditions met on
the shores of the Gulf of Mexico. The result of this meeting was fatal
to one of them, although the day was fraught with auguries for both.

To the Christian army under Hernando Cortés the day had especial
significance. They named the place where they went ashore Villa Rica
de Vera Cruz (The Rich Town of the True Cross). They thereby neatly
combined the twin passions that controlled the actions of the expedition – gold and souls.

To the ambassadors of the great native monarch, Moctezuma, who
arrived the following day, the year of the meeting had a singular
significance. According to the Aztec calendar, based on a recurring
fifty-two-year cycle, it was a year called Ce Ácatl (One Reed). Long
centuries before, the god Quetzalcoatl had told them that he was born
in a year with that designation and that he would return to them from
his home in the eastern seas in another year Ce Ácatl.

Quetzalcoatl had come from the east. Hernando Cortés had come
from the east. The ambassadors returned to the great city of Tenochtitlán and told their emperor that the god had returned. The priests of
Quetzalcoatl accepted the word. Had they but known the text, the
priests might well have reflected later in their Spanish torture cells and
prisons on the words in St. Mark's Gospel:

Then if any man shall say unto you, Lo here is the Christ, or there, believe it not. For there shall arise false Christs and false prophets, and shall show great signs and wonders; insomuch that (if it were possible) they shall deceive the very elect.

2

The meeting between the civilizations of Europe and America was one of the most dramatic encounters in recorded history. The differences between the two civilizations were profound. Neither had any prior knowledge of the other. There was no common heritage – at least none that was apparent in that first confrontation. They saw the planetary environment with different eyes, they experienced the sense of beauty in different ways, and they interpreted that experience in terms that were mutually exclusive. It was a cultural shock of the first magnitude, whose echoes have not yet died away.

For the Mexicans, the meeting was immediately traumatic. A legend came to life, an ancient prophecy was fulfilled in a terrifying manner. The horse, a native of the Americas which had become extinct long aeons before the establishment of the first native cultures, had returned, bearing on its back a bearded, god-like type of man armed with steel sword and lance. The horse and rider, thought at first to be one creature, were more frightening than the death-dealing muskets the Spaniards also carried.

For their part, Cortés and his hard-bitten campaigners had never in their lives seen anything like the power and splendour of the Aztec state. One of them, Bernal Diaz del Castillo, averred that there were cities in Mexico "greater than any in Spain." Considering that the population of Seville at that time was less than 100,000, while the Aztec capital of Tenochtitlán and its environs was home to one million citizens, the *conquistador* can scarcely be accused of exaggeration. The great New World city was in fact far larger than any of the great cities of Europe. London did not reach the quarter-million mark until the seventeenth century, while the population of Paris in 1594 was only 180,000, and Rome was a provincial capital of less than 100,000.

The first sight of the great city of Mexico stunned the Spaniards. Diaz says:

> During the morning, we arrived at a broad Causeway and continued our march towards Iztapalapa, and when we saw so many cities and

villages built in the water and other great towns on dry land and that straight and level Causeway going towards Mexico, we were amazed and said that it was like the enchantments they tell of in the legend of Amadis . . . . And some of our soldiers even asked whether the things we saw were not a dream. It is not to be wondered at that I here write it down in this manner, for there is so much to think over that I do not know how to describe it, seeing things as we did that had never been heard of or seen before, not even dreamed about.

It is not to be wondered at either that the descriptions left by Diaz and others are not more detailed. The tall pyramids, the brightly painted temples and colleges, the barbaric beauty of the costumes of the priests and nobles – these were things to be taken in at the corner of the eye. The Spaniards were soldiers; they were only 400 in number and their objective was conquest and loot.

Much has been written about the meeting between Cortés and Moctezuma and its tragic aftermath. Unfortunately for his people, Moctezuma was more priest than warrior, more poet than autocrat. An ascetic and visionary, he received Cortés with generous hospitality, at first convinced that he was dealing with the deified Quetzalcoatl himself, or at the very least, an emissary of the god. According to Diaz, this was made quite clear at the first encounter between the two men in Moctezuma's great palace. Moctezuma is quoted as saying:

Long time have we been informed by the writings of our ancestors that neither myself nor any of those who inhabit this land are natives of it, but rather strangers who have come to it from foreign parts. We likewise know that from those parts our nation was led by a certain lord . . . who then went back to his native land, where he remained so long delaying his return that at his coming those whom he had left had married the women of the land and had many children by them and had built themselves cities in which they lived, so that they would in no wise return to their own land nor acknowledge him as lord; upon which he left them. And we have always believed that among his descendants one would surely come to subject this land and us as rightful vassals.

This is but one account of what Moctezuma said at that fateful meeting. There are others, and few agree. What does emerge, however, from all accounts is that Moctezuma unequivocally accepted the role of vassal to Cortés' liege lord, Charles V, King of Spain and Holy Roman Emperor, and that this acceptance was based on an ancient prophecy.

The Aztec emperor never altered this stand, despite the unethical behaviour of the Spaniards and the defection of many of his own people and tribes allied to them. He paid for his loyalty to the ancient legend with his own life, at the hands of his own people.

After Moctezuma's death, the people of Tenochtitlán arose and drove the strangers out of their city. The Spaniards returned, their numbers augmented by hordes of native warriors belonging to tribes which had long chafed under the harsh Aztec system of tribute, and the last great native civilization of Mexico was destroyed – "beheaded . . . as the passer-by sweeps off the head of a sunflower."

3

On August 15, 1521, Hernando Cortés completed his conquest of the Aztec empire. His victorious troops marched into the blackened, blasted, and bloody ruins of what had been one of the mightiest cities on earth. That night, by the flickering light of a thousand fires, a tremendous storm descended on Tenochtitlán. Thunder shook the skies and bellowed over the waters of the lake on which the city was built. Screaming gales howled down the long avenues between the temples, the schools, and the market places. The priests of Quetzalcoatl, cowering among the overthrown and shattered stones of their sanctuaries, recalled that the Feathered Serpent was also the god of the winds.

Even before the city fell the Spanish priests were puzzling over the legend of the god or hero whose ancient prophecy had so facilitated the conquest. It was discovered that the god's name was made up of two words in the Nahuatl language spoken by the Aztecs – *quetzal*, a tropical bird of brilliant plumage, and *coatl*, meaning either serpent or twin. The excitement that this discovery elicited was for a while intense, as the priests remembered that the Apostle Thomas was also called *Didymus* (in Greek, a twin).

The character of Quetzalcoatl, as revealed in these early dialogues with the natives, did much to reinforce devout speculation as to his possible Mediterranean Christian origin. The faith he had taught the people was a gentle one. There seemed to have been much emphasis on good deeds, love, and brotherhood. Flowers were offered on the altars of the temples instead of blood sacrifices and symbolic butterflies represented the human soul.

This ideal picture proved to be as evanescent as the span of a butterfly's life. The gentle faith of Quetzalcoatl, it appeared, had been taught in theological colleges by priests whose hair and fingernails were clotted with the blackened blood of the tens of thousands of victims – as many as 20,000 on a single occasion, it was said – whose living hearts were torn out in sacrifice to other gods of the blood-burdened Aztec pantheon.

The dichotomy was too extreme for the Spanish priests to stomach. Revulsion set in. The works of the native priesthood and all their gods – including Quetzalcoatl – were assigned to Satan and his legion of devils. An intense drive for the salvation of the souls of the poor deluded Mexicans was embarked upon with all the fervour and many of the methods of the Holy Inquisition.

A necessary part of the campaign to overthrow and destroy the native beliefs and replace them with the sixteenth-century Spanish version of Christianity was the destruction of the native scriptures. Some of the societies that the Spaniards discovered were literate and possessed many written records dealing with history, science, and religion. No one knows how many of these works were obliterated in the first fine flame of Christian nihilism.

Fortunately there were a few Spanish friars whose education placed them above the level of the commonalty of unlettered country padres. Included in this number were Bernardino de Sahagún, Juan de Torquemada, and a repentant Diego de Landa, who in a Spanish prison cell tried to rectify the consequences of his *auto-da-fe* of the Mayan books by writing a history of the people of his diocese. These men, along with a select group of Christian-educated native aristocrats like Don Fernando de Alva (Ixtilxochitl) and Alvaro Tezozomoc, tried to capture the form and texture of a dying civilization and dying faith before it was too late. Foremost in this company of the wise was Bernardino de Sahagún (1499-1590). This Franciscan monk who worked among the Aztecs compiled what has been called the earliest scientific ethnographic investigation of any people. The techniques he employed in preparing his monumental *Historia general de las cosas de Nueva Espana* (General History of the Things of New Spain) were above reproach. First, he sought out the most learned men and got them to set down, in Aztec pictographic writing, what they remembered of their history, religion, and legend. Then he asked other natives who had been taught the Roman alphabet in the mission schools to transcribe the pictographs into Roman characters but in the Nahuatl tongue. Then, having learned the Aztec language himself, he compared the results to detect any errors or fabrications.

Like most students of pre-Columbian Mexico, past and present, Sahagún was fascinated by the strange, ubiquitous figure of Quetzalcoatl. His succinct summation of the character of the hero-god has been echoed by many a scholar since:

> Quetzalcoatl was . . . the greatest figure in the ancient history of the New World, with a code of ethics and love for the sciences and the arts.

However, the deeper Sahagún probed into the story of Quetzalcoatl, the more confused the picture became. To begin with, Quetzalcoatl was not originally a god of the Aztecs. In their semi-barbarian days, when they had swept down into the Valley of Mexico from the north, they had adopted him from an earlier people – the Toltecs, whose great, half-mythical capital was Tula. This was made clear in the epic *Song of Quetzalcoatl*, from which a few significant verses are here quoted:

> All the glory of the godhead
> Had the prophet Quetzalcoatl;
> All the honour of the people.
> Sanctified his name and holy;
> And their prayers they offered to him
> In the days of ancient Tula.
> There in grandeur rose his temple;
> Reared aloft its mighty ramparts,
> Reaching upward to the heavens.
> See, his beard is very lengthy;
> See, exceeding long his beard is;
> Yellow as the straw his beard is.

> And his people, they the Toltecs,

Wondrous skilled in all the crafts were.
All the arts and artifices
So that naught there was they knew not;
And as master workmen worked they.

. . .

And in Quetzalcoatl all these
Arts and crafts had their beginning;
In him all were manifested.
He the master workman taught them
All their arts and artifices.[1]

Where was this Tula? Who were these Toltecs?

These were questions that not even the wisest Aztec priest could answer. It had all happened a very long time ago. Tula and the Toltecs had disappeared even before the Aztecs had created their first settlement at Tenochtitlán in 1325 A.D. The mystery of Quetzalcoatl's capital and people was not solved until the 1940's.

Further research, first by Sahagún and later by Juan de Torquemada and others, revealed Quetzalcoatl of Tula to be an even stranger figure than had at first been supposed. Some of the elements of the legend bore a queer resemblance to the Christian doctrine of the Trinity. Quetzalcoatl's mother, Chimalman, was a virgin. God, the All-Father, appeared to her one day in his guise as Citlallatonac, "the morning." He breathed on her and she conceived.

One cannot completely disregard a suspicion that some elements of the Quetzalcoatl epic may have been invented for the benefit of the Spanish priests. It is in fact extremely difficult to be absolutely certain of the dating of parts of the story of the hero-god.

Other aspects of the Toltec legend carry no hint of Christian influence. There is an account of a prolonged duel between Quetzalcoatl and his dark brother, Tezcatlipoca, "the smoking mirror," which has a tragic ending. Tezcatlipoca gives the aging Quetzalcoatl a magic potion and makes him look at himself in a mirror. Overcome by the sight and drunk with his brother's poison, Quetzalcoatl sends for his sister, Quetzalpetlatl, makes her drink of the cup, and they lie together. Four days later, crushed by his shame, Quetzalcoatl parts from the people he has ruled for twenty years and sets out for the Red Land, the Dark

Land, the Land of Fire. These are names anciently applied to the peninsula of Yucatan.

Into this account one may read a national memory of the conflict between the invading Aztecs and their precursors in the Valley of Mexico – between the priesthood of the invaders and an older established faith. It is a story old in human history and it ends as all such stories end – with the assimilation of the old god into the enlarged pantheon of the conquerors.

The adoption by the Aztecs of this strange god into their horrendous Olympus placed almost intolerable strains on the patterns of their religious thought. The gentle Quetzalcoatl, the teacher, philosopher, and prophet, walked uneasily in the company of Huitzilopochtli, god of war and the sun, drinker of blood, and the demoniacal Coatlicue, goddess of earth and of death, the licker of skulls. In the result, the same priests who fed Huitzilopochtli bleeding hearts and Coatlicue raw skulls placed spring flowers on the altars of Quetzalcoatl. The same people who gathered in tens of thousands to watch the corpses tumbling down the steps of the temple-pyramids tended with loving care the floating gardens of Tenochtitlán. It is a strange picture; one that Calvin might have dreamed and Breughel might have painted, but neither would have fully believed in.

This same terrifying spiritual and philosophical dichotomy is found almost everywhere in Middle and South America where the legend of the hero-god found firm footing, although never quite as extravagantly developed as among the Aztecs. It permeated and shaped the art of Middle America, which, as Paul Westheim has pointed out, is spiritually oriented and symbolically stated.[2]

4

As time went on and succeeding generations of scholars puzzled over the legend of Quetzalcoatl, it became clear that the lost city of Tula was not the only place associated with the legend. There were other "cities of Quetzalcoatl." Cholula was one. There, a vast pyramid, covering forty-five acres and rising to a height of 210 feet, a more monstrously large construction than even the great pyramid of Khufu, in Egypt, was said once to have been crowned by Quetzalcoatl's temple.

Cholula still lived when Cortés arrived. It was a great city then, an important one, a Mecca for the faithful. So important was it, that it was once facetiously said that the Spaniards built 365 churches there in an attempt to smother the cult of Quetzalcoatl. That is not so, but it is a fact that more Christian churches were erected there than the population of the city could ever have justified.

According to the local version of the epic of the hero-god, he came to Cholula after leaving Tula. Following a reign of an additional twenty years, he left Cholula for the coast, embarking on a raft of serpents for his eastern home. Still another version of the departure says that he had his attendants build a funeral pyre, on which he threw himself. While his body burned his heart ascended and after four days appeared in the skies as the planet Venus. All accounts end with his promise to return in a year Ce Ácatl.

While students continued to probe the apparently endless threads of the legend, still another "city of Quetzalcoatl" slumbered in unrecognized antiquity. The ruins of Teotihuacán lie some thirty miles northeast of Mexico City. The site is so large and the surviving structures so imposing that it was one of the earliest archaeological areas to attract the attention of the Spanish priests. Yet they built no great churches there. There was no need to do so. Whatever native cult had been practised there had long since vanished. When Bernardino de Sahagún questioned the natives they would say only:

> It is called Teotihuacán. And when the rulers died, they buried them there. Then they built a pyramid over them . . . and they built the pyramids of the sun and moon very large, just like mountains. It is unbelievable when it is said they are made by hands, but giants still lived there then.

All memory of the builders of this great and beautiful city with its huge pyramids, temples, public buildings, colleges, broad avenues, and splendid vistas was gone completely. Over the years a theory developed that this must have been the ancient Tula, so closely associated with the name of Quetzalcoatl. Indeed, some recent guidebooks of Mexico still so identify it. Today, however, thanks to the research that has been carried on intermittently at the site since 1905, it is known that Teotihuacán was already more than 1,000 years old when Quetzalcoatl of Tula reigned over the Toltecs.

By the middle of the nineteenth century, research had revealed so many confusing and contradictory aspects of the Quetzalcoatl legend that the whole story had fallen into disrepute among serious scholars who were now inclined to dismiss the whole thing as a "solar myth" – that handy grab bag into which the practical Victorians thrust almost any folk legend that was not demonstrably Christian. A further factor in the degradation of the epic was the wholesale use of it by the inhabitants of the "lunatic fringe." The story was to them a godsend. It was used by Joseph Smith and the Mormons to solve the mystery of the missing tribes of Israel. Quetzalcoatl was identified by enthusiastic amateurs – and even by some addled professionals – as the Irish St. Brendan, the Welsh King Madoc, a Norse adventurer, and as an emissary from the Lost Continent of Atlantis or the Land of Mu.

It was an American researcher, Daniel G. Brinton, who first tackled the problem of the Quetzalcoatl legend scientifically. Brinton performed an invaluable service by unravelling the tangled skeins of the legend to reveal not one Quetzalcoatl, but two. In summary, he discovered that the legend could be separated chronologically and geographically into two distinct stories. In the first, far back in time, a figure known as Quetzalcoatl was credited with being the first father, a lawgiver and civilizer. A cult was established with him as the central figure. This cult continued to flourish for centuries and the high priests of the cult frequently called themselves after the god, Quetzalcoatl.

One such high priest who (as often was the case among the Mexicans) was also ruler of his people, reigned at a place called Tula (or Tollan) at a time roughly corresponding to the tenth century of the Christian era. He was known as Quetzalcoatl. The epic that Sahagún received from the Aztec priests was largely his story.

Since Brinton's time, this theory has been expanded and refined to the point where this second, legendary Quetzalcoatl, the priest-king of Tula, has assumed full historical perspective as a real, once-living person. His name was Topiltzin, and he was born in a year Ce Ácatl. He was a priest of the Quetzalcoatl cult and as such bore the full title: Our Prince Topiltzin Ce Ácatl Quetzalcoatl. During his reign there was trouble at Tula – apparently a revolt against his religious teachings. He left his city with some of his followers and, after spending some time in the land of the Mixtecs, made his way to the coast of the

Gulf of Mexico, from which he set sail on "a raft of serpents."

Whether Topiltzin-Quetzalcoatl used a raft of snakes or some more conventional conveyance, he and his followers are next found in the peninsula of Yucatan among the Maya. The date was 987 A.D. They built a new Tula at the Mayan city of Chichén Itzá where Topiltzin became known as Kukulcan, a straight Mayan translation of the Nahuatl Quetzalcoatl.

Nearly 200 years later Tula was destroyed by invaders, and Huemac, the last king of the Toltecs to rule there, migrated with the remnants of his people to Yucatan where they arrived about 1191. Huemac is said to have died in 1208, being buried in the strange oval pyramid known as the House of the Sorcerer at Uxmal.

But what of the earlier Quetzalcoatl – the original Quetzalcoatl from whom Topiltzin took his name and title? Modern archaeological research has linked the worship of Quetzalcoatl to the ancient site of Teotihuacán and to a period a thousand years before the heyday of Tula.

Teotihuacán is an entirely different kind of city from most whose ruins are found in Middle America. With the possible exception of Dzibilchaltún in Yucatan, most of the so-called "cities" of the high cultures were in reality ceremonial centres serving extended areas of a largely rural population. Teotihuacán was a true city in the European sense, supporting and serving an urban population of not less than 100,000 at its peak.

Teotihuacán is unique in other ways as well. The huge structures that dominate the site today were apparently erected during a single building operation during the earliest phase of the occupation of the site "at a time when no structures of comparable size were being built anywhere else in Middle America or in the rest of the New World." [3] The date that has been assigned to the largest edifice – the Pyramid of the Sun – is between 100 A.D. and 200 A.D.

So remarkable was this sudden flowering of a huge, complex, urban centre that many writers have postulated the introduction of a foreign influence to account for it. There are arguments on both sides of this position. What is agreed by all, however, is that the building of the Pyramid of the Sun must have been inspired by a powerful and living faith. According to the legendary sources such a faith was that inspired and taught by Quetzalcoatl.

Teotihuacán is the oldest of the so-called "cities of Quetzalcoatl."

The separation of the hero-god legend into two chronological strata resolves part of the problem of the identification of its origins, but still leaves us faced by a rather intimidating paradox. Both Quetzalcoatls – the early Quetzalcoatl of Teotihuacán and the later Quetzalcoatl of Tula – represent sophisticated religious concepts. Yet the symbolical representations of the hero-god throughout Middle America show a barbaric plumed serpent with savage jaws agape.

Why would a hero who taught love and brotherhood and believed in the sacrifice of fruit and flowers rather than human flesh be shown under such a fierce mask? This can be explained without too much difficulty if we assume a still earlier cult of Quetzalcoatl – a primitive, anthropomorphic, totemistic cult, represented by a dragon-like, non-human, serpent figure. The development of such a cult is entirely compatible with what we know of the beginnings of the American native cultures. As the examination of the mythologies of other primitive societies throughout the world demonstrates, the emergence of a totemistic religion of this type is quite natural. On the other hand, the sudden emergence of a moralistic religious concept like that of Quetzalcoatl of Teotihuacán must be considered as highly unusual.

Traces of the practices of this hypothetical ancient, archaic, and primitive cult of Quetzalcoatl can be found woven throughout the popular religions of the Middle American civilizations up to the time of Cortés, and they undoubtedly included human sacrifice. Such a cult would not be easily overthrown. It would have had centuries of development behind it. Any new faith would have had to make compromises with the practices of the old, just as St. Paul's Gentile Christianity made compromises with paganism. The late Miguel Covarrubias, one of those who supported the theory that the second-century florescence of Teotihuacán was due to the influence of a foreign element, noted that such an élite would have had "to make important concessions to the existing culture of a large, established population."[4]

Just as Prince Topiltzin of Tula took the name of Quetzalcoatl of Teotihuacán, Quetzalcoatl of Teotihuacán may have taken the name of the principal pagan deity of that place. If this hypothesis is correct – and the work of Daniel Brinton and others strongly supports it – then there are three levels within the Mexican legend of Quetzalcoatl:

1. Vestiges of an early religious cult based on the worship (or at least symbolical use) of a totem representing a snake – probably a rattlesnake – bearing a plume of feathers from the quetzal bird.

2. The figure of a man – a ruler and priest – who was later deified but may in the beginning have been accepted as the living personification of a tribal, totemistic deity. This man is associated with the foundation of the city of Teotihuacán in the second century A.D.

3. Prince Topiltzin, ruler and high priest of the city of Tula in the tenth century A.D., who took the name of his predecessor, was driven out of his city, and journeyed with some of his followers to the Mayan area in Yucatan where he died.

The difficulties confronting the student trying to unravel the tangled threads of the Quetzalcoatl legend can be understood when it is realized that fifteen centuries elapsed between the establishment of the cult and the first modern European encounter with it. During those centuries, Europe suffered a Dark Age – the near-extinction of classic civilization. In that same period, Middle America endured three such eclipses of learning. The first came with the violent destruction of Teotihuacán in the sixth century A.D. This was part of a general upheaval throughout Mexico which apparently led to the overthrow of the faith of Quetzalcoatl and the introduction of a warrior cult.

Three centuries later the great cities of the Mayan Classic Period in Mexico and Guatemala were abandoned by their citizens and left to the mercies of the jungle. This is one of the great mysteries of pre-Columbian America. One of the theories advanced to account for the desertion of these temple-centres with their amazing pyramids and palaces supposes that there was a popular revolt against the priest-rulers resulting in a state of anarchy. It is to this theory that I personally subscribe.

The Toltec prince, Topiltzin, revived the cult of Quetzalcoatl for a brief time in the tenth century, only to be driven out by another warrior cult. Two centuries later the Toltec empire collapsed, leaving a devastated land. This is graphically described by C.A. Burland in his *The Gods of Mexico*. Burland explains the historical purpose of the myth of Quetzalcoatl and his "dark brother," Tezcatlipoca, in the light of this catastrophe:

After the fall of Tollan [Tula] there was no central government anywhere in Mexico. Some of the Toltecs escaped . . . and founded a new city far away at Chichén Itzá, but on the plateau of Mexico the old civilization broke down completely. Famine and pestilence followed the civil war and by the end of this terrible time the country was nearly depopulated. The legends give us a picture of miserable survivors living in small half-abandoned towns, most of the population dead through famine, and a long period of slow reconstruction in front of the survivors . . . .

To those who survived it must have seemed that the world had come to an end. Memories of the disaster remained until the coming of the Spaniards in the form of fantastic folklore about how Tezcatlipoca, the black magician, had changed his form to lure the Toltecs to their doom. People did not like to talk about the war, so this magician was depicted as a being who led the Toltecs out from Tollan and caused mountains to fall on them, or else he appeared as a great giant who suddenly became a rotting corpse and spread disease among them, apparently out of a spirit of pure mischief.

The next great native power to appear in Mexico was that of the semibarbarian Aztecs. When they founded their city of Tenochtitlán in 1325, the Aztecs established their own warrior cult and the worship of their terrifying war god Huitzilopochtli. To him and other equally bloodthirsty gods of their pantheon were added Tezcatlipoca and his gentle brother, Quetzalcoatl. The efforts of the Aztec priesthood to blend these widely diverse elements into a single state religion were grotesque in the extreme.

From this brief survey it will be seen that the cult of the "humble, virtuous and peace-loving" Quetzalcoatl was under attack almost from its inception by the priesthoods of the old gods, the invasions of barbarian tribes, and the ardour of the masses for the old superstitions. When all this is considered, the survival of the cult, its beliefs and its practices, as well as the memory of its founder through 1,500 years, is little short of miraculous. It is no wonder the threads of the legend are tangled. That it did persist for such a long span of years, through so many vicissitudes over such a vast area, gives some indication of the power of the influence exerted by the person of Quetzalcoatl of Teotihuacán.

Chapter Two

ITZAMNA AND KUKULCAN

Where there was neither heaven nor earth sounded the first word of God. And he unloosed himself from his stone, and declared his divinity. And all the vastness of eternity shuddered. And his word was a measure of grace, and he broke and pierced the backbone of the mountains. Who was born there? Who? Father, thou knowest; he who was tender in heaven came into being.

— *The Chilam Balam of Chumayel.*

1

When Cortés and his *conquistadores* encountered the Aztecs, they met a native civilization at the peak of its powers. In the peninsula of Yucatan, Cortés' lieutenant, Francisco de Montejo, found only the shattered remnants of what had once been the greatest of all American civilizations – the Mayan.

This once mighty people, whose accomplishments have caused them to be called by many scholars "the Greeks of the New World," had fallen on evil times. After the abandonment of the great cities of the first period of their history in the ninth century, the Maya turned their civilizing energy to the construction of a group of new cities in the northern part of the peninsula. There was a cultural renaissance, interrupted by the invasion of the Toltecs under their king, Huemac, in 1191. The conquerors introduced an alien form of government, the principal feature of which was centralized authority. A new city – Mayapán – was built as the capital. It was the only walled city in the Mayan territory. A confederation of three city-states – Chichén Itzá, Uxmal, and Mayapán – was attempted. This ushered in nearly two centuries of struggle for power, both among the newcomers and against them. Finally, widespread civil war led to the destruction of Mayapán in 1441 and the end of centralized authority. In 1464 a devastating hurricane ravaged the peninsula, followed in 1480 by a plague which carried off thousands. Thus, by the time Montejo arrived the Maya had been reduced to a state of near-anarchy.

However, since the Maya had had only a brief experience with the kind of federal authority characteristic of the Aztecs, their religious and civil practices continued to function after a fashion in many of the larger centres. The priesthood continued to serve the temples, to maintain the calendar and the astronomical observatories upon which the accuracy of the calendar depended, and to record their observations in their sacred books.

The city-state form of government in Yucatan proved, somewhat paradoxically, to be a better defence against Spanish aggression than Aztec absolutism. When Moctezuma and Tenochtitlán fell, so did the entire Aztec empire. Mayan Yucatan had to be subjugated city by city. The last large centre of Mayan resistance was not conquered until 1697. The territorial district now known as Quintana Roo was, in fact, never brought under Spanish rule. Its native inhabitants finally made a treaty with the Mexican federal government in 1925, since which time they have been officially citizens of the Republic of Mexico.

On his way to the conquest of Mexico, Hernando Cortés met the Maya twice – once on the east or Caribbean coast of Yucatan and once on the western or Gulf coast. He was met with hostility on both occasions despite the fact that the Maya, like the Nahuatl peoples, had a legend about an earlier visit to their land of a white, bearded culture hero.

The mighty city of Tenochtitlán was already only a memory when the Spaniards again turned their attention to the geographically isolated peninsula of Yucatan. The king of Spain awarded the governorship of the province to Francisco de Montejo. He had first, of course, to subjugate the inhabitants. It proved to be a task that occupied the rest of his life and part of that of his son and successor, Francisco de Montejo the Younger.

The chief opposition to the Spanish "civilizers" came from the ranks of the Mayan priesthood, for the government of the city-states would appear to have been theocratic in nature. It was not force of arms that finally reduced the Maya to serfs, but the force of Christian ecclesiastical authority. The Montejos, in true *conquistador* fashion, pulled down the temples. But it was a Franciscan friar, Diego de Landa, who pulled down the faith that nourished the altars. Fray Diego de Landa (1523-1579) spent twenty-three years among the Maya before being elevated to the bishopric of Yucatan in 1572. During those years he learned much about the religion of the people. Especially he learned the importance of their sacred books to the priesthood. In the as yet undeciphered Mayan hieroglyphs, the priests entered calendarical and astronomical calculations and recorded their history and their religious beliefs.

A literate society is vulnerable through its writings. If all the Bibles in the world were simultaneously to be removed from circulation, Christianity would not be destroyed but it would certainly be seriously crippled. The Franciscan zealot laid his plans with painstaking care. By one means or another he caused to be gathered together all the available Mayan books at a village called Mani – which appropriately means "the end." There, in July 1562, they were burned.

The *auto-da-fé* at Mani was one of the most tragic events in history – more tragic than the burning of the great library at Alexandria in 47 B.C. After all, many of the Alexandrine titles existed elsewhere in copies distributed throughout the ancient Mediterranean world, but the complete works of a civilized, literate society were destroyed forever at Mani. Of the unknown number of scientific, historical, philosophical, and religious books that existed in Yucatan prior to 1562, only three books survive.

This was a shock from which the already badly battered Mayan culture never recovered. The lamentations of the people were heartbreaking and touched even de Landa. The so-called "jaguar priest" or *chilam balam* of Tizimin recorded the anguish of the Maya in words strongly reminiscent of the lament of the Jews of the Babylonian captivity (Psalm 137):

> With rivers of tears we mourned our sacred writings amid the delicate flowers of sorrow in the days of the katun. Vale.

The Christian authorities at home in Spain were apparently more tolerant of the native religious beliefs than some of their priests in the missionary field. In any event de Landa was summoned back to give an account of his cure of souls in Yucatan. While there, under detention, he wrote his apologia, *Relacion de las Cosas de Yucatan*.

Ironically, de Landa's account "of the things of Yucatan" is today the source of much of our knowledge of the Mayan civilization as it was encountered in its decadent stage by the Spaniards. Indirectly de Landa and the other Spanish friars working in the area also made possible the salvaging of some of the Mayans' knowledge of the past. In their efforts to Christianize and "civilize" the Indians, the priests taught them to transpose their own language into Spanish so that they could more quickly absorb Christian teachings. Inevitably, their students used the new knowledge to record what they could remember of their ancient heritage. A few of these post-Conquest documents have survived. Chief among them are: The *Popul Vuh,* a collection of the myths and history of the Quiché-Maya of Guatemala; *The Annals of the Cakchiquels*, a similar record also from Guatemala, and the so-called *Books of Chilam Balam*, written in Yucatan by various priest-scribes.

From a study of these and other sources, both native and Spanish, there emerges a legendary figure similar in many respects to the Mexican Quetzalcoatl. The destruction of so many records, the savagery of the Church's treatment of the priesthood, and the fragmentary nature of the remembered events combine to create a confusing and confused picture. Like the Nahuatl legend, the Yucatecan story proved to be a complex of two different legends dating from two different historical periods. In the earlier legend the central figure was someone called Itzamna. The later hero was called Kukulcan. It is now not difficult to identify the second culture-hero. He is the previously discussed Prince Topiltzin, the priest of Quetzalcoatl. He is remembered in Yucatan by the name Kukulcan, which is a direct translation into Mayan of "the feathered serpent." Whether the Kukulcan of the Maya was in fact the exiled prince of Tula or a descendant calling himself by the same name or title is impossible to determine, but the source of the influence is unmistakable. His capital was the old and abandoned Mayan city of Chichén Itzá. Here the stranger and his followers erected buildings, sculptures, and columns of a type duplicated in only one other place in Middle America – at ancient Tula.

The late Herbert Joseph Spinden, a leading Mayan scholar and archaeologist, professed a great admiration for Kukulcan, identifying him by his Nahuatl title as "emperor" of the Toltecs and assigning to his achievements specific dates in the Christian calendar:

Quetzalcoatl, emperor of the Toltecs, and conqueror of the Mayas – priest, scientist and architect in one commanding individual – was a contemporary of Henry II and Richard the Lion Hearted. He died in far off days before a reluctant King John signed the Magna Charta of English liberties. His holdings in Mexico and Central America

32

were several times more extensive than the holdings of those puissant monarchs of the Angevin line in France and the British Isles, his philosophy of life was richer and his contributions to the general history of civilization were greater than theirs. Old stone walls in eastern Yucatan are mute evidence of the commerce, religion and art that Quetzalcoatl built up as the expression of his practical and ideal State. He encouraged trade that reached from Colombia to New Mexico, he preached a faith of abnegation and high ethics which later led speculative churchmen to identify him with St. Thomas, and in sculpture and architecture he formed a new and vital compound of the previous achievements of two distinct peoples, the Toltecs of the arid Mexican highlands and the Mayas of the humid lowlands. We can restate three of Quetzalcoatl's personal triumphs in astronomical science corresponding to the years 1168, 1195 and 1208. We know that he conquered the great city of Chichén Itzá in 1191 and erected therein a lofty temple which still bears his name and a round tower which is still an instrument for exact observation of the sun and moon. We know that Quetzalcoatl set up a benign system of local self government among conquered tribes of Guatemala which made those peoples relate his praises in song and story. We know that after his death he was made a god because during his life he had been "a great republican!" [1]

Some twenty years after writing these words, Dr. Spinden claimed to have established that Kukulcan died in the building known as the Temple of the Magician at Uxmal on the evening of April 4, 1208, and that the great observatory at Chichén Itzá was a memorial to him, dedicated on the seventy-second anniversary of his death, April 4, 1280.

Whether or not Spinden's calculations were correct, the fact remains that few serious students now dispute the historicity of Yucatan's Kukulcan. It is widely accepted that he was a real historical personage and not a mythological figure. Certainly it was in that light that he was viewed by the Maya, who told Bartolome de Las Casas, an early priest-explorer, that, "in ancient times there came to that land twenty men, the chief of whom was called Cocolcan . . . . They wore flowing robes and sandals on their feet, they had long beards and their heads were bare. They ordered that the people should confess and fast."

The confessional rite as observed in Yucatan was probably much like that of the Aztecs, as noted by Sahagún. He says confession and absolution were available only once during a penitent's lifetime. The words of absolution are reported in this manner:

> Oh brother, thou hast come to a place of great danger, and of much work and terror . . . thou hast come to a place where snares and nets are tangled and piled one upon another, so that none can pass without falling into them . . . these are thy sins, which are not only snares and nets and holes into which thou hast fallen, but also wild beasts, that kill and rend the body and the soul . . . by thine own will and choosing thou didst become soiled . . . and now thou hast confessed . . . thou hast uncovered and made manifest all thy sins to our lord who shelters and purifies all sinners; and take not this as mockery, for in truth thou hast entered the fountain of mercy, which is like the clearest water with which our lord god, who shelters and protects us all, washes away the dirt from the soul . . . now thou art born anew, now dost thou begin to live . . . .[2]

To conclude this brief account of the Kukulcan cult, it remains to note that the figure carved on the doorpost of the stone temple topping the great pyramid at Chichén Itzá, said to represent Kukulcan, is tall, commanding, wears a long, flowing robe and has an aquiline nose and a long beard.

2

The Christian missionary practice of converting pagan shrines to places of Christian pilgrimage and worship has already been commented upon. The holier the place, the more ambitious the Christian foundation. A prime example of this technique is, of course, Cholula.

It is significant that no serious attempt was ever made to supplant or suppress the cult of Kukulcan. The present church at Chichén Itzá is a small unpretentious building of Spanish colonial vintage. There are no great ecclesiastical foundations at Uxmal, at the ruins of Mayapán, nor even at Mani, where the descendants of Huemac's warrior aristocracy still ruled in de Landa's time.

The one really monumental Christian religious foundation in Yucatan was established at Izamal, a small village midway between Merida and Valladolid. The huge priory complex there was begun in 1549 and remains today one of the largest church buildings in the Americas. It was a Franciscan foundation; and until 1949, at least, there was a small group of monks and teaching brothers in residence there.

Diego de Landa became prior of Izamal in 1553 while building was still in progress. It was here that he learned much of what he later incorporated into his *Relacion de las Cosas de Yucatan*. It was quite clear that Izamal was for the Maya a very holy place. The site was old. Five great towering pyramids brooded over the village. De Landa was told that one of them – torn down to make way for the priory – was the burial place of Itzamna, sometimes known as Itzamna Canil.

Who was this Itzamna – god or man?

What de Landa and others discovered about him can best be summarized in the words of Crescencio Carrillo, a scholar of the last century:

> To this ancient leader, Itzamna, the nation alluded as their guide, instructor and civilizer. It was he who gave names to all the rivers and divisions of land; he was their first priest, and taught them the proper rites wherewith to please the gods and appease their ill-will; he was the patron of the healers and diviners, and had disclosed to them the mysterious virtues of plants . . . .
>
> It was Itzamna who first invented the characters or letters in which the Maya wrote their numerous books, and which they carved in such profusion on the stone and wood of their edifices. He also devised the calendar, one more perfect even than that of the Mexicans, though in a general way similar to it. Thus Itzamna, regarded as ruler, priest and teacher, was, no doubt, spoken of as an historical personage, and is so put down by various historians, even to the most recent.[3]

From this it can be seen that Itzamna was looked upon as a man, an historical personage, at least by the Mayan priesthood and intelligentsia. It would appear, however, that in time he came to be deified in the minds of the common people. In the surviving Mayan codices he is represented, in profile, as an old man with but a single tooth and a little pointed beard.

De Landa made other discoveries at Izamal which emphasized the peculiar and important nature of the site:

> While the friar, the author of this book, was in this country, they discovered in a building which they destroyed, a great urn with

three handles with silver-coloured flames painted outside and enclosing the ashes of a burned body with some arm and leg bones of a marvelous size, and three fine beads of stone of the same kind which the Indians use for money.

Alfred M. Tozzer, author of the best English translation of de Landa's *Relacion*, commented on this burial:

It seems to have impressed the early Spaniards. Landa speaks of it three times and there are passages in several of the early *Relaciones*, evidently referring to the same cremation.

Another unusual feature of the Izamal complex were two gigantic stone heads, which engaged the attention of several nineteenth-century travellers. In 1839 John Lloyd Stephens saw one which was approximately eight feet high by eight feet wide. Désiré Charnay saw it in 1863 and remarked on the beauty of the workmanship which he said was quite unlike the sculptures found at Palenque and other Mayan sites. When Charnay returned to Izamal in the 1880's this head was gone, quarried by the natives for building materials, but he found a second "great stone face" which was thirteen feet high, at the base of the same mound. When Alfred Tozzer visited the site in 1902, only a small part of the stucco covering of the face remained. This, too, had disappeared by 1929 when Phillips Russell went to Izamal.

More durable memorials of the Itzamna cult are the observations made by de Landa and other Spanish friars on the nature of the religious beliefs and rites followed by the ancient priesthood. To begin with there seems to have been a basic and widespread belief in a single creator god who was not identified with Itzamna. No temples were erected in his honour, no idol depicted his likeness "for no man knew what he looked like." He was known as Hunab Ku, which has been translated as the "one true god" (Mayan: *hun* – one; *ab* – state of being; *ku* – god).

A distinction must be made here between the beliefs of the ruling classes and those of the commoners. The concept of a supreme deity remote from human affairs was obviously not one that recommended itself to a population of farmers and artisans concerned with the mundane matters of rainfall and sunshine, the direction of the prevailing winds on the trade routes, and the influence of the phases of the moon on the growth of crops. The cult of Hunab Ku was probably never any more popular with the Mayan masses than was Moses' monotheism with the tribes of Israel. Just as Yahweh's attributes – mercy, anger, wrath, compassion – were always more easily understood than the being of God Himself, so the attributes of Hunab Ku's creation – the rain, the winds, the sun and the moon – were more easily comprehensible and hence more easily worshipped than the godhead himself.

It is these attributes of creation that constitute the so-called Mayan pantheon. Generally speaking, the "gods" are related to the forces of nature. Their characteristics are markedly dualistic – the rain was benevolent when it brought needed moisture, malevolent when it brought hail to batter the crops. Each aspect of each god was worshipped, or propitiated, individually.

The Mayan priests were also skilled astronomers and mathematicians. They had an almost obsessive preoccupation with numerical values, being in this respect one of the most sophisticated of all peoples. It is perhaps not surprising therefore to discover that they considered all the various aspects of creation – rain, the sun, good and evil – as being at the same time separate, but one. The idea compares with the Christian doctrine of the Trinity but on a greatly expanded scale.

It must again be emphasized that such complex religious beliefs were probably the exclusive field of the priesthood. De Landa and others among the first generation of Christian priests to serve in Middle America captured some of the flavour of advanced Mayan religious thought. They had the advantage of discussing these matters with surviving members of the intellectual élite.

By the time modern anthropologists began making a study of the beliefs of the ancients, all that was left were the folk tales, the myths, and the nursery stories passed on verbally by the common folk. If our knowledge of Christian doctrine were to be based only on the popular hagiology of the Middle Ages, we would be left with an entertaining literature but with no true concept of the complex nature of God as seen by the Jewish people and exemplified in the life of Jesus.

To turn from the beliefs of this ancient people, the true nature of which must be at least partly speculative, to the rites by which they expressed their beliefs, we are on slightly firmer ground. De Landa, like Sahagún, reported practices that at first encounter resembled Christian rituals. Confession and absolution were administered by the priests. Indeed, the Mayan language had one word for "soul" and one for "purged soul." There was also a rite of baptism, but it was not given to infants, only adults. A major difference seems to have been that in many instances baptism, confession, and absolution were available only immediately prior to death. De Landa also noted traces of a sacred, communion-like meal.

3

We have seen that in Mexico proper and in Yucatan there existed a two-layered account of a foreign cultural hero. We have seen that in both places these figures were widely separated in time. In both places they were considered to be not gods, but men – at least in the beginning. Their characters are similar. The earlier visitor is a teacher, the latter a priest, king, and warrior. Their teachings are similar in both areas.

There are certain significant differences between the Mexican and the Yucatecan legends. In Mexico, the early Quetzalcoatl leaves his adopted people to return to his distant homeland. Quetzalcoatl-Topiltzin abandons his city of Tula, goes to the Gulf Coast and embarks on his raft of serpents, promising one day to return.

In Yucatan, the teacher, Itzamna, dies and is buried in a great pyramid at Izamal which becomes a holy place, a place of pilgrimage. Kukulcan-Topiltzin also dies in Yucatan.

In Mexico, the white, bearded Cortés was received at first with honour and reverence by a people who took him to be the returning hero. In Yucatan, Cortés' lieutenant, Francisco de Montejo, was greeted with determined hostility. Is it not likely that this was so because the Mayan legend contained no prophecy of a return? Montejo could not be Kukulcan for that conqueror of the Maya lay long mouldered. He could not be Itzamna for all knew that the head, the heart, and the healing hands of the great teacher were enshrined at Izamal.

No matter where the stories of Quetzalcoatl and his successor, the Prince Topiltzin, began, they both ended in Yucatan.

Chapter Three

VOTAN

At some indefinitely remote epoch, Votan came from the far east. He
was sent by God to divide out and assign to the different races of men
the earth on which they dwell, and to give to each its own language. The
land whence he came was vaguely called *valum votan*, the land of
Votan. His message was especially to the Tzendals.

— D.G. Brinton, *American Hero-Myths.*

1

The city of Quetzalcoatl was Teotihuacán. The city of Itzamna was
Izamal. The cities of Prince Topiltzin, the priest of Quetzalcoatl, were
Tula and Chichén Itzá. The city of Votan was Palenque.

Palenque is an archaeological site in a heavily jungled area in the
Mexican state of Chiapas. It was one of the largest cities of what is now
called the Mayan "Classic" period. The earliest deciphered dated monument records a date equivalent to 642 A.D. Palenque is Spanish for
"palisade" and was the name given to the site when its existence was
reported by an Indian to a Spanish priest in 1773. Its ancient Mayan
name is unknown. While the total area of the ancient city is still not
known, despite many years of excavation, piles of rubble representing
collapsed structures extend at least three and a half miles in one direction and two miles in another from the principal ceremonial complex.

It was clear from the beginning that Palenque, apparently abandoned in the ninth century A.D., had been a very important religious
centre. In fact its importance was known to Europeans long before its
existence was reported to them.

2

Towards the close of the seventeenth century, the Bishop of Chiapas,
Nuñez de la Vega, came into the possession of a book written in the

Tzendal language (a regional Mayan variant). The book, purported to be written by one Votan, told the story of himself and the origin of his people. Votan, a name said to mean "heart" in Tzendal, had come from the east by divine command to found a settlement at what is now known as Palenque. Setting out from the land of Chivim, he passed by the "dwelling of the thirteen snakes," arrived at a place called after himself, passed through the island-strewn Laguna de los Terminos, on the Gulf Coast of Yucatan, south up the Usumacinta River and on one of its tributaries, the Otolum River, founded Palenque.

The newcomers were at first looked upon with suspicion by the natives who called them *Tzequil*, petticoated, from the long, flowing robes they wore. Later, however, they changed their views of the colonists and "soon exchanged ideas and customs with them, submitted to their rule, and gave them their daughters in marriage."

Four times Votan returned to his ancestral home, the land of Chivim. Returning from the first of these voyages he came upon a tower which had been planned to reach the heavens but was destroyed because of a "confusion of tongues" among its builders. Prior to each return voyage he divided the country into four districts, placing over each one of his own men. In one of these districts, that known as Huehuetlán, Votan put a treasure consisting of lidded clay jars, green stones, and many stone portraits in a damp, dark, subterranean house. A woman was appointed to guard the treasure.

Votan did not die, like ordinary mortals. When his time came he descended through a cave into the underworld and so found his way to "the root of heaven."

Unsatisfying as it is, we know little more about the contents of the book of Votan. Its European discoverer, Bishop de la Vega, and another Spaniard, Ordonez de Aguilar, copied out a number of extracts from the book, which remain now the source of our information concerning it.

Then, in 1691, following the clues contained in the book, Bishop de la Vega sought out and found Votan's treasure at Huehuetlán, still guarded by a priestess. At his pre-emptory command she surrendered the contents of the building. Then in an impressive ceremony in the market-place of the town, the looted treasure was publicly burned along with the only surviving copy of Votan's book as well as other manuscripts.

Long before a Mayan priest-prophet had given the people forewarning of such dark days:

On that day, a blight is on the face of the earth,
On that day, a cloud rises,
On that day, a strong man seizes the land,
On that day, things fall to ruin.

3

Like the story of Quetzalcoatl, the legend of Votan stirred much interest in the nineteenth century and led to much speculation. Many attempts were made to identify the racial origins of the man and to locate the places mentioned in the account of his voyage from his homeland.

The Phoenicians were an early and perhaps natural choice for the romantic speculators of the last century. This fascinating and somewhat mysterious folk had had a well-deserved reputation as the greatest navigators and travellers of the ancient Mediterranean world. They have been credited with trading voyages beyond the pillars of Hercules to Britain, the Shetland Islands, and even Iceland.

The adherents of the theory of a Phoenician origin for Votan and his followers even ventured to identify places mentioned in the account of his great voyage and to assign an approximate date for it. Chivim was Canaan or the Chittim of the Old Testament which was Cyprus, a Phoenician colony. The "dwelling of the thirteen snakes" was the thirteen Canary islands off the coast of West Africa. The land of Votan was either Cuba or Hispaniola. The reference to the great tower was taken to refer to the Tower of Babel – in other words, Babylon. Since the great temple at Babylon was in fact being rebuilt by Nabopolassar and his successor Nebuchadnezzar in the seventh and sixth centuries B.C., it was to this construction that Votan's account referred. The speculators did not try to explain how a voyager on the Mediterranean could "come upon" the temple of Babylon many miles distant from the sea on the banks of the Euphrates River.

One early writer, Pablo Cabrera,[1] claimed that the Phoenician inscriptions on two marble columns found long ago at Tangier, Morocco, actually traced the route of Votan. This is out of keeping altogether with the normal Phoenician practice of jealously guarding the secrets of their trade routes from potential commercial rivals.

The dress of the strangers – the long, flowing robes which caused them to be called *tzequil* – was identified by the speculators as typical Phoenician garb. They conveniently overlooked the fact that such dress could equally be attributed to the Greeks, the Romans, or any civilized Mediterranean nation of the Old World.

The Phoenician theory of the origin of Votan has recently been revived in a more sophisticated fashion by Constance Irwin[2] and other writers. Their reasoning is ingenious but like the nineteenth-century speculators, they fail to take into account the powerful current of religiosity and ethical philosophy which permeates the cults of Quetzalcoatl, Itzamna, and Votan. The pre-eminence of such considerations in the tales of these men can hardly be imputed to Phoenician seafarers and traders of the sixth or seventh centuries before Christ.

4

The resemblances between the legend of Votan and those of Quetzalcoatl and Itzamna are self-evident. Although there are no specific references to beards, Votan and his followers came from a remote land across the eastern seas, dressed in an odd fashion and introduced many new ideas.

To arrive at even an approximate date for the origin of the Tzendal legend is difficult if not impossible, thanks to the burning zeal of Bishop Nuñez de la Vega who destroyed evidence that might have provided at least a clue. However, if Votan's legendary role as the founder of Palenque is accepted, archaeological evidence would imply a date not later than 642 A.D., and probably much earlier. The earliest deciphered, dated Mayan monument, *in stone*, at Palenque carries that notation, and there is some evidence that earlier dates were recorded on more perishable material, such as wooden slabs. This date is too late for Quetzalcoatl of Teotihuacán and probably for Itzamna of Izamal as well, and it is too early for Prince Topiltzin of Tula and Chichén Itzá.

There are certain possibilities. One is that the legend of Votan was imported by the Tzendals from the north, from Izamal, or from the west, from other regions of Mexico. This seems unlikely in view of the wealth of circumstantial detail about the wayfarer and his followers. Another possibility is that the story relates to still another group of seafarers from the homeland of Quetzalcoatl or some other place across the seas. The most likely possibility is that Votan was a descendant of the earlier immigrants. A German writer, Johann Georg Müller, reported in the middle of the last century a Mexican myth which suggested that Votan was grandson of Quetzalcoatl.[3]

In any case, Votan is in the great tradition of Quetzalcoatl and Itzamna – a stranger who exerted a powerful influence on the religious thought, art, and poetry of the civilized native peoples of Middle America. Although Votan, long after he passed from the scene, was credited with the invention of writing and all manner of civilized practices, modern archaeology shows this to have been mere hyperbole. The peoples to whom Votan, Quetzalcoatl, and Itzamna came were already far along the road of civilization. The huge structures they had built throughout Mexico and Middle America, their sophisticated mathematical system, their accurate astronomical observations, all indicate that a high degree of technical excellence was achieved a considerable time before Quetzalcoatl embarked on his massive program of urban renewal at Teotihuacán in the first half of the second century A.D.

The influence these men had on the indigenous civilizations was not technical, but religious and philosophical. Irene Nicholson,[4] who identifies (mistakenly) Quetzalcoatl, Kukulcan, and Votan as the same individual, expresses the great sense of loss that every student in this field experiences:

It is a universal tragedy that we know so little of this great religious leader, Quetzalcoatl-Kukulcan-Votan: plumed serpent, quetzal bird, Venus and sun god, who sacrificed himself that true manhood might be created in the hemisphere of the west.

The same writer has also feelingly described the enormity of the task confronting those who would learn more about this great leader and the elusive reward that such a search may one time grant the fortunate searcher:

In spite of the great gulf that separates pre-Columbian thought from our own in many of its external aspects; in spite of distortions, irrelevancies, decadence and subsequent annihilation by European conquerors of a great part of it; the culture which this mysterious leader established shines down to our own day. Its message is still meaningful for those who will take the trouble to make their way, through the difficulties of outlandish names and rambling manuscripts, to the essence of the myth.

5

An echo of the Votan legend was found among the Zoques, a lowland coastal tribe who were in rather close contact with the Tzendals of the highlands. From the Tzendals they received, in attenuated form, some of the religious ideas of the more advanced peoples of Mexico. Their hero legend, as reported by D.G. Brinton, had strong parallels with the Votan of the Tzendals:

> This myth relates that their first father, who was also their Supreme God, came forth from a cave in a lofty mountain in their country, to govern and direct them . . . . They did not believe that he had died, but that after a certain length of time, he, with his servants and captives, all laden with bright gleaming gold, retired into the cave and closed its mouth, not to remain there, but to reappear at some other part of the world and confer similar favours on other nations. The name, or one of the names, of this benefactor was Condoy.[5]

Chapter Four

GUCUMATZ AND HURACÁN

There were only immobility and silence in the darkness and in the night.
Alone was the Creator, the Maker, Tepeu, the Lord, and Gucumatz, the
    Plumed Serpent, those who engender, those who give being, alone
    upon the waters like a growing light . . .
Then light came while they consulted together; and at the moment of
    dawn man appeared while they planned concerning the produc-
    tion and increase of the groves and of the climbing vines, there in
    the shade and in the night, through that one who is the Heart of
    the Sky, whose name is Huracán.

– From the *Popol Vuh*.

The *Popol Vuh* is an account written some time after the Spanish conquest by an unknown Quiché-Maya Indian of Guatemala. It purports
to be the reconstruction of a lost narrative of the distant past. While
many of the best passages are sonorous and dignified, much of it consists of anthropomorphic folk tales similar to those long current
among American tribes. There are legends concerning the celestial
origin of maize, a creation myth (part of which is quoted at the head of
this chapter), and an account of how the animals were denied the
privilege of coherent speech.

Nevertheless, there are in the *Popol Vuh* dim and muted memories
of the great gods of the temple centres of Yucatan. There was a chief
god, Hunapú, who was a twin. He was the god of the hunt; his twin
was Ixbalanque, whose name means "little jaguar." Together the twins
fought the power of evil represented by Vucub-Caquix, whose aspect
was shining and beautiful but whose heart was full of sin.

Then there is Gucumatz, a stranger and wanderer, whose name
means plumed or feathered serpent. He is sometimes identified with
Ixbalanque, the jaguar god, in which guise he was said to have descended into the underworld to combat the enemies of mankind and
particularly, of course, the enemies of the Quiché-Maya. On his return,
expecting to be honoured by them, he received instead surliness and
ingratitude. In anger he left them forever, "to seek a nobler people."

Gucumatz did not reside among the Quichés, apparently merely visiting them from time to time. His adventure in the underworld was said to have taken place to the eastward, in the Guatemalan province of Verapaz. There may be a clue in this. There was in this area in ancient times a large and important Yucatecan Mayan trading station. Gucumatz may well have been that "Feathered Serpent" known in Tula as Prince Topiltzin and in Yucatan as Kukulcan. Topiltzin or his successor, Huemac, is said to have wielded authority over a very large area, to have knit the Mayan-speaking tribes together as no other ruler had, and to have promoted trade with other peoples. His visits to the Quichés may have been in the nature of official tours. Their "ingratitude" may represent a refusal to enter Kukulcan's political federation of Mayan cities or to pay tribute to one claiming suzerainty over them.

The third great name in the *Popol Vuh* is that of "the great lord, Huracán." Some scholars trace an affinity between Huracán and the Mexican Tezcatlipoca, the opponent and tempter of Quetzalcoatl. He is often shown in an opposing position vis-a-vis Quiché human heroes. His, however, was a post of supreme authority, punishing the wicked and rewarding the just. His home was across the seas and references to sea voyages recur frequently in the legend. Huracán's name meant "heart of heaven." One is reminded immediately that Votan's name also meant "heart," in much the same sense.

If Gucumatz and Huracán are memories of real persons, then Huracán, as the senior hero, can probably be equated with Itzamna or Votan and Gucumatz is Prince Topiltzin or his successor. There is always the possibility, of course, that the Quiché heroes were not the original strangers but their descendants, just as Votan was said to be the grandson of Quetzalcoatl. But neither Gucumatz nor Huracán are especially remembered as being fair or bearded.

Chapter Five

BOCHICA AND NAYMLAP

North of Peru, the Muysca Indians of the plain of Cundinamarca in Colombia had a legend of one called Bochica, a white man with a beard, who appeared suddenly among them, while savages, and taught them how to build and sow, and formed them into communities, settling their government.

— F.A. Allen, *Polynesian Antiquities.*

Last in the cavalcade of South American strangers is a flamboyant creature called Naymlap. Different in tone, the legend of Naymlap . . . provides a glittering picture of an immigration in process, as the natives believed that their forefathers had actually witnessed it in Lambayeque, a Peruvian province which lies along the Pacific.

— Constance Irwin, *Fair Gods and Stone Faces.*

1

Neither the legend nor the person of Quetzalcoatl seem to have made any lasting impression on the jungle tribes of Central America south and west from Guatemala to the land mass of South America. Since no native civilizations developed in this area, there was no civilized vehicle to transmit the story of the wanderings of the hero. Nevertheless, there are here and there traces of the cult and a few artifacts pointing to its existence.

Once within the zone of the high cultures of the Pacific coast of South America, the legend reappears and proliferates to an extent second only to its incidence in Middle America.

Geographically, and probably chronologically as well, it appears first in the plains area surrounding Bogotá, the capital of Colombia. The legend had its origin in the second and third Christian centuries. I suggest therefore that the figure of Bochica (or Bohica) can be equated with that of Quetzalcoatl of Teotihuacán and Itzamna of Yucatan. In appearance, Bochica was white and bearded; in character, benevolent Appearing suddenly among the Muyscas or Chibchas, he was credited with having taught them all they knew. D.G. Brinton[1] drawing on a work by Lucas Fernandez Piedrahita in 1688[2] says this of Bochica:

47

He came from the east, from the llanos of Venezuela or beyond them . . . . His hair was abundant, his beard fell to his waist, and he dressed in long and flowing robes. He went among the nations of the plateaux, addressing each in its own dialect, taught them to live in villages and to observe just laws. Near the village of Coto was a high hill held in special veneration, for from its prominent summit he was wont to address the people who gathered round its base. For many years did he rule the people with equity, and then he departed, going back to the East whence he came, said some authorities, but others averred that he rose up to heaven. At any rate, before he left, he appointed a successor in the sovereignty, and recommended him to pursue the paths of justice.

Like other native nations who played host to the hero-wanderer, the Chibchas or Muyscas attributed their pre-eminence in the cultural arts to Bochica. Archaeologically, this legendary statement is not borne out by the facts. Before the time at which Bochica was assumed to have visited them, they had already advanced far on the road to high culture. For more than a thousand years before the coming of the Spaniards, these tribes had enjoyed a higher living standard than most of their neighbours. They lived in large timber houses, used coins – round tiles of gold with no stamp or markings – mummified their dead, and bore their chiefs on litters.

As is typical wherever the legend is found, the hero was known by many names, some of them obviously symbolical. He was also called Xue, Nemterequetaba, Zuhe, or Sua. *Sua* was the ordinary word for sun, which gratified Daniel Brinton, serving thereby to strengthen his theory that the legend was a sun myth.

When the light-skinned Spaniards arrived in Colombia, they were assumed to be the envoys of Bochica and were addressed as *Sua* or *gagua*, another word for sun.

2

The legend of Bochica reports that he came to the Chibchas or Muyscas from the llanos of Venezuela "or beyond them." It is no surprise therefore to learn that east of the Andes, in Venezuela, Paraguay, and Brazil, there are legendary accounts of a venerated traveller who was called Tsuma, Tamu, Tume, or Zume.

The early Spanish explorers and priests reported that wherever the widespread Tupi-Guarani race extended – from the mouth of the Rio de la Plata and the boundless plains of the Pampas, north to the northernmost islands of the West Indian archipelago – they were told tales of a venerable and benevolent old man to whom the tellers attributed their knowledge of the arts of life and whom they called "Our Ancestor."

In Paraguay the traveller was called Pay Zume, *pay* being a word meaning magician, prophet, or priest. He came in the remote past from somewhere in the east and was remembered as a living man, not as a god. As usual in these legendary accounts he came eventually to be credited with the invention of agriculture and especially with having taught the people the difficult art of processing the poisonous manioca plant into an edible food.

Some of the reported events of his life echo those in the legend of Bochica. According to the Paraguayan story, Zume used to mount an elevation near the city of Assumption, around which he gathered his people while he delivered to them his instructions and his laws. There is an echo here as well from some of the legendary accounts of Quetzalcoatl. It is said that the Mexican hero used to follow the same practice from the summit of the mountain Tzatzitepec, "The Hill of Shouting."

Other aspects of the Zume legend follow the familiar pattern. He lived for a certain length of time with his adopted people and then left them. Some accounts say he went back over the ocean to the east. Other stories say the people rebelled against his rule and drove him to the bank of a river where they fired arrows at him. The culture-hero caught the arrows in his hand, magically and, with the aid of his divine powers, walked across the river on the water and disappeared from their view in the distance.

There are no consistent references to Zume as having been either white or bearded but in all other essential respects his legend parallels the other stories.

3

West of "Bochica country" on the Pacific coast, in the Peruvian province of Lambayeque, there exists a legend about a wandering hero and his company of quite a different sort. The legend is much later than the Bochica story and has become interwoven and intermixed with the tale of the earlier hero in a fashion familiar to us by now from the Middle American accounts.

The stranger's name was Naymlap. The circumstantial tradition records also the names of many of the forty principal people who formed his "royal" court, including his chief wife, Ceterni (he had many secondary wives, or concubines). The immigrants, landing at the mouth of a river called Faquisllanga, moved a short distance inland to build their first town and to erect a temple to which they gave the name *Chot* .

Naymlap founded a dynasty that endured for eleven generations. The names of the successive rulers of the line were still well enough remembered to be reported verbatim to the Jesuit priest Miguel Cabello de Balboa in the middle of the sixteenth century.

Naymlap was no missionary bearer of a new faith, but a secular leader seeking for a new people to govern. He did not teach and pass on, as did Bochica and the other manifestations of the early hero. He stayed to rule and to establish the sovereignty of himself and his successors over a subject people.

The story of Naymlap is strongly reminiscent of the accounts of Prince Topiltzin of Tula, the Kukulcan of Yucatan. Indeed, several German scholars, including W. Lehmann, Walter Krickeberg, and E.W. Middendorf, have pointed to distinct archaeological parallels. Thor Heyerdahl, in his *American Indians in the Pacific*, has quoted Lehmann:

> Balboa's account of Naymlap and his company and successors shows certain conformities with Toltec tradition. This has been pointed out by Krickeberg too . . . . The Chot temple which Naymlap built is probably preserved in the stepped pyramid which lies about four kilometres from Eten and to the left of the road leading to Reque. It was about this pyramid that Middendorf early remarked that it most resembled the buildings in Central America and Mexico.

This persistent, secondary, and almost certainly later legend, which occurs in many of the same areas where the earlier legend is more dimly enshrined, must have a basis in historical fact. What that fact may have been is not my concern in this book, which is an attempt to untangle the origins of the legend of that Quetzalcoatl who was the builder of Teotihuacán. My purpose in citing these other accounts is to draw a distinction between two levels of legend, often intermixed and confused not only by European scholars but by the native Americans who reported them, but which are in fact widely separated in time.

The Bochica legend distinctly refers to the beard worn by the hero; I have come across no references citing a similar appearance for Naymlap.

Chapter Six

VIRACOCHA AND THUNUPA

O Pachacamac Viracocha, Thou who showed favour to me for so short a time, and honoured me and gave me life, dost Thou see that I am treated in this way, and seest Thou in Thy presence what I, in mine, have seen and see?

— Prayer of the Sapa Inca, *Huáscar.*

1

The conquest of Peru was a replay of the conquest of Mexico. All that is needed is to substitute the names of Francisco Pizarro for that of Hernando Cortés; Atahualpa for that of Moctezuma; and Viracocha for that of Quetzalcoatl.

Francisco Pizarro, a one-time Spanish swineherd, first saw the coasts of Peru in 1527. What he saw aroused his cupidity, and in 1532 he returned with 180 free-booters to claim his own kingdom on earth. Within a year he was master of an empire with a population of 3,500,-000 people living in an area approximately equal to that of the thirteen British colonies at the time of the American Revolution.

His victory was an even greater one than that of his fellow-country-man, Cortés. The people he defeated, named after the title of their ruler, the Inca, lived under a much more tightly knit system than that of the Aztecs. The Inca empire was a despotic welfare-state in which the destiny of every individual was rigidly controlled from the cradle to the grave.

The empire, extending for 2,500 miles along the Pacific coast of South America, including much of what is now Ecuador, Peru, Bolivia, and Chile, was linked in its various parts by a well-engineered road system fully the equivalent of the ancient Roman system and vastly superior to the European roads of the sixteenth century. Along the roads, on which couriers passed and repassed with the business of empire, were huge irrigation projects, temples, pyramids, post-houses, and teeming cities. Of one town, Pachacamac, near modern Lima, an unlettered Spanish *conquistador* said: "It is larger than Rome."

Yet 180 sweaty, bearded, raunchy Spanish brigands overturned this complex, civilized national entity in a matter of months. How did they do it? By the power of a legend more than a thousand years old.

2

Atahualpa, the Inca, or emperor, was resting at the resort town of Cajamarca when runners brought word of the landing of the Spaniards. The reports were accurate as to the number of men in the party. However the Spaniards' horses confused them. At first they identified horse and rider as one beast. A second report corrected this misinformation. The horses were said to be a kind of sheep. The newcomers were fair and bearded.

This last piece of information delighted Atahualpa. He had just won a bitter civil war against his brother, Huáscar, and was preparing for a triumphal entry into the capital, Cuzco. Now came this great good omen. Only the gods were white and wore beards. Long years before the greatest of the gods, Viracocha, white and bearded, had departed from these coasts, promising to return one day to his adopted people.

Viracocha or his envoys had returned and would lead the Inca Atahualpa, sole ruler of the "four quarters of the world," into his capital city. The sign was unmistakable. Atahualpa awaited the arrival of the gods.

The "gods" soon showed their cloven feet. It was reported to Atahualpa that a party of the newcomers had raped a number of the sacred Virgins of the Sun in their convent at Cazas. Although the perpetrators of this sacrilegious act were instantly punished by their commander, Hernando de Soto, the image of the Spaniards as envoys of the gods had suffered an irremediable setback. These were no gods but men; heathen invaders.

Atahualpa was no religious ascetic like Moctezuma. He was a man of action, a warrier. His army, so lately victorious over the forces of Huáscar, was with him. Let the foreigners come. They would receive a hot reception.

Francisco Pizarro entered Cajamarca on November 15, 1532. The town, with a normal population of 10,000, was deserted. Unknown to

Pizarro, the Inca had ordered it cleared, in order to provide accommodation to his Spanish guests. Atahualpa, with his army, was encamped a short distance away. No embassy met the strangers. It has been suggested that Atahualpa intended to put the Spaniards in their place and show them that they were not very important.

Pizarro sent Hernando de Soto as emissary to the Inca's camp to request a meeting at Cajamarca. The Inca, consumed with curiosity and confident in his own military superiority, consented. The meeting took place on Saturday, November 16, in the great military parade ground at Cajamarca. There was only one entrance to the square. In late afternoon the Inca arrived, borne on a litter of solid gold, preceded by hundreds of sweepers cleansing the path for the "Lord of the World." Accompanying him was the royal guard, in sky-blue livery studded with gold, silver, and jewels. They were followed by some 6,000 members of the court and the army, all unarmed as for a ceremonial occasion.

Not a single Spaniard was in sight.

Atahualpa demanded to know where the foreigners were.

Hard on cue, a Dominican friar, Vicente de Valverde, appeared, bearing a Bible in one hand and a crucifix in the other, accompanied by an interpreter.

Through the interpreter, Valverde briefly explained the Christian faith and the purpose of the Spanish expedition which was, he said, to convert unbelievers and to bring them to acknowledge Charles, King of Spain and Holy Roman Emperor, as secular liege lord and the Pope as Vice-regent of Christ on earth and supreme arbiter of men's souls.

With understandable pique, the Inca declared that he was no man's vassal. As to the Pope, he thought he must be mad "to talk of giving away countries which do not belong to him." As to the faith of which the friar spoke, he found it lacking in reason:

> Your own god, as you tell me, was put to death by the very men he created. But my god still looks down upon his children.

He then took the Bible, which the friar had quoted as his authority for these extraordinary claims, and contemptuously hurled it to the ground.

The friar picked up the Bible, hurried to the well-hidden Pizarro and cried, "Fall on at once! I absolve you!"

Pizarro waved a white scarf, the agreed signal for attack, and hell broke loose. Two cannon belched death into the square. Fifty guards burst upon the multitude, slashing and hacking with sword and lance, followed by the Spanish infantry discharging thunder and fire from their murderous muskets. The single entrance to the square was blocked by other Spaniards who killed so many the pile of dead removed the necessity for further service there. The panic-stricken crush of Inca bodies collapsed a hundred-yard section of stone and adobe wall. The Spanish cavalry pursued the escapees and butchered them. By sunset, three to four thousand unarmed Peruvians were dead and the Inca was a Spanish prisoner.

Atahualpa's life, put in escrow by treachery, was preserved, temporarily, by greed. With the sacred person of the emperor as hostage, Pizarro demanded and got the largest ransom ever collected in the history of extortion. A room at Cajamarca, twenty-two feet long by seventeen feet wide, was to be filled to a depth of nine feet with gold. Another smaller room was to be filled, twice over, with silver. The wealth of the empire was ransacked to provide the ransom. The temples, the roofs of many of which were tiled with gold, the images of the gods themselves in their inner sanctuaries, public buildings, and convents were stripped of ornamentation to fill the treasure rooms at Cajamarca. The silver room was filled and the gold room had approached the nine-foot mark when the flow of loot began to dwindle. Bored with his cat-and-mouse game with the emperor and hoping, perhaps, that a final act of cruelty would spur the frightened populace into more speedy compliance with his wishes, Pizarro determined to dispose of the Inca.

In August 1533, Atahualpa was tried before a hastily convened court and convicted of the crime of heresy – of refusing to accept the merciful god of the Christians. He was sentenced to a heretic's death – burning alive at the stake. Father Valverde, playing the role of Job's comforter, again appeared on cue and offered the Lord of the World an easier death by the garrote, if he would accept the Christian rite of baptism.

Atahualpa accepted. He made the responses and gestures required, which to him were meaningless, and was baptized Juan, since it was August 29, the feast day of St. John the Baptist.[1] Then the executioner slowly tightened the knotted rope about his throat until the lifeless body of the last Inca slumped against the stake.

The Dominican friar, Vicente de Valverde, won his bishop's mitre by his fanatical campaign for the conversion of the "pagan" Peruvians. His greatest triumph was the baptism of the Inca. He was not so successful with other members of Atahualpa's court. The Inca's principal general, Chalcuchima, is said to have refused the Christian rite under torture and to have died in agony at the stake with the name of Pachacamac on his lips.

Who was Pachacamac?

He was God – creator of the universe and animator of men's souls. He was remote, unknowable, unapproachable, and almighty.

Viracocha was his emissary.

This relationship was not immediately apparent to the European conquerors and their ecclesiastical advisers. It is still not clear to many modern archaeologists and anthropologists. It was not really understood by the Incas, who used the names Pachacamac and Viracocha interchangeably as synonyms for the "All-Father."

The Incas, like the Aztecs, were comparative newcomers among the civilized peoples of the Americas. Before 1200 A.D. they were Stone Age savages, living probably in the region of Lake Titicaca, two miles above sea level. They were nomads, hunters, and part-time farmers. By the fourteenth century – the same century in which the Aztecs founded Tenochtitlán – they had learned enough of the civilized ways of the peoples they had conquered to found the Inca dynasty.

The Incas worshipped the sun and his sister-bride, the moon. It may be worth noting here that the astronomical-astrological cult, which became common throughout Middle and South America, is now considered by most scholars to have been a late development in the religious patterns of the Americas. It is likely that the identification of Quetzalcoatl in Mexico and Viracocha in Peru, as the planet Venus, dates to this late period.

As conquerors and assimilators of culture, the Incas acknowledged and absorbed the religion of their predecessors and superiors. From the lowland tribes, anciently influenced by the great civilization of the Mochica culture, they adopted the worship of Pachacamac. From the people of the highlands, from the old and mysterious culture of Tiahuanaco, they took the worship of Viracocha. As their empire grew in material and spiritual sophistication, the twin cult of Pachacamac-Viracocha became the pre-eminent religious force while the cult of the sun and the moon slipped to a subsidiary position.

The religion of the pre-Columbian Peruvians baffled and infuriated the Spanish friars. There was, first of all, Pachacamac, the creator-god. There was a belief in an after-life, rites of purification by water, confession, absolution, and penance. There was a story of a universal flood, and there were prayers, equal in piety and submission to a universal Will to the best in European Catholicism:

> O Creator! O conquering Viracocha! Ever present Viracocha! Thou who art in the ends of the earth without equal! Thou who gavest life and valour to men, saying, Let this be a man! and to women saying, Let this be a woman! Thou who madest them and gave them being! Watch over them that they may live in health and peace. Thou who art in the high heavens and among the clouds of the tempest, grant this with long life, and accept this sacrifice, O Creator.[2]

Pachacamac, in the pantheon of the Inca and pre-Inca peoples, never appeared as anything but disembodied spirit. Viracocha, on the other hand, was a man – a white man with a beard. He was of imposing appearance. of medium height, and he wore a long, flowing robe. His name means "Sea-Foam." He appeared, a stranger, on an island in Lake Titicaca. He and his followers built the great, strange, and ancient structures at Tiahuanaco. He taught the peoples of that place sculpture, engineering, architecture, irrigation, and terrace farming. Finally, spurned by his adopted nation, he descended to the coast and sailed westward out over the Pacific Ocean, promising that some time in the future he would send envoys further to protect and teach them.

4

Pachacamac was a universal god, impersonal and impossibly remote from the affairs of men. Viracocha was a human figure from the very ancient past, a teacher, civilizer, and "first father." Another legendary figure was Thunupa (also called Tonapa or Taapac). He was a missionary. Harold Osborne in his *South American Mythology* (Hamlyn Press: 1968) summarized the Thunupa legend in this manner:

> Thunupa appeared on the Altiplano in ancient times, coming from

57

the north with five disciples. He was a man of august presence, blue-eyed, bearded, without headgear and wearing a *cusma*, a jerkin or sleeveless shirt reaching to the knees. He was sober, puritanical and preached against drunkenness, polygamy and war. He first came carrying a large wooden cross on his back to Carapucu, the capital of the famous chief Makuri, and reproved the latter for his warlike deeds and his cruelty. Makuri took no account of him, but the priests and soothsayers set up an opposition to him. Thunupa then went to Sicasica, where his preaching annoyed the people and they set fire to the house where he was sleeping. Escaping from the fire, Thunupa returned to Carapucu. But during his absence one of his disciples had fallen in love with and converted the daughter of Makuri, and on his return Thunupa had her baptized. Angered at this, Makuri martyred the disciples and left Thunupa for dead.

Some versions of the legend tell of Thunupa's escape from the wrath of Makuri; others tell of his death and burial at Cochamarca or Arica, on the Pacific coast near the border between Chile and Peru. It is told that his enemies tried unsuccessfully to destroy his cross. His memory was still green when the Inca Roca was baptized with water from a spring which Thunupa had consecrated. In the time of Roca's successor, the Inca Capac Yupanqui, a house in which Thunupa had lived was ordered preserved as a shrine.

From these legendary accounts a rough chronological sequence may be formulated. The cults of Pachacamac and Viracocha pre-date by many centuries the advent of the Inca founders on the *altiplano*. Pachacamac would seem to have an affinity with the ancient Mochica civilization of the first centuries of the Christian era and the faith taught by their culture-hero, Bochica. Bochica, it will be remembered, was white and bearded, like Viracocha, benign and dressed in a long, flowing robe. There is no mention of a cross in either the Bochica or Viracocha legends.

Thunupa, although he was white and bearded like the other two, dressed differently and carried a wooden cross. He was not as successful as either Bochica or Viracocha in his task of conversion, and he had an unfortunate habit of laying curses on those who rejected his teachings. He was well enough remembered in the days of the Incas for the house in which he lived to be identified. Unlike Viracocha, he died in South America and the place of his burial was known at least approximately.

When all these factors are added together it becomes obvious that Thunupa belongs to a much later date than Viracocha or Bochica. It is more than possible therefore that he was roughly contemporary with Prince Topiltzin of Tula or one of his successors, while Viracocha is a figure from an earlier period.

Significantly, Viracocha is closely identified with the ancient site of Tiahuanaco on Lake Titicaca, on the border between modern Peru and Bolivia. The civilization that developed there, beginning in the early centuries of the Christian era, influenced a very extensive area in South America.

PART II

THE
ARCHAEOLOGICAL
EVIDENCE

Chapter Seven

THE GREAT AWAKENING

At some point, before the invasion of sun worship, religious thought
appears to have developed into pure monotheism and the concept of an
impersonal god, if not in the mass of the people, then in individual cases
of priests and seers.

— Hermann Leicht, *Pre-Inca Art and Culture.*

From the accounts in the foregoing section it will be seen that the
general tenor of all the hero legends is essentially the same. All deal
with the same or a similar event. Many of the similarities are remarkably consistent, the most outstanding being that in all instances the
visitors were aliens to the peoples they visited. Indeed on the basis of
these similarities some writers have advanced a thesis that all the legends are local variants of a single story – in other words, that it was the
epic that did the travelling, not the heroes of the epic. I cannot for a
moment entertain this theory in view of the weight of the evidence
against it; at the same time I believe that the story, in attenuated form,
did eventually reach peoples who had had no personal contact with the
culture-heroes themselves.

Now we must inquire more fully into the basic premise of this book
– that the legends in fact derive from historical events in the history of
the Americas.

The true history of these continents prior to the Spanish conquest
has yet to be written. What we know is not history but a collection of
orally transmitted myths and legends, a small collection of books
(many of them written in hieroglyphs still not fully deciphered), numbers of calendrical inscriptions on stone, and the work of two or three
generations of archaeologists and their interpreters.

Here and there native records of varying degrees of authenticity
provide us with fairly detailed accounts of kings, priests, and events.
Nearly all are of late date. The last two centuries of Aztec rule, for

instance, are reasonably well documented. Our knowledge of the last century or so of the remarkable Inca empire comes near in detail to what we know of the last years of Roman rule in Britain. The great events in the history of the Maya peoples from 1191 to the advent of the Spaniards are known to us in broad outline. Before the twelfth century, however, all is darkness. What we know of the Americas prior to that time is almost entirely dependent on what we can discover from the material remains of cities, towns, temples, and camp-sites.

We who share a common European heritage are apt to dismiss as inconsequential that which is out of the mainstream of so-called "Western culture." In doing so we overlook the fact that much of our heritage lies in the same kind of historical limbo as that of the Americas. Our debt to the ancient Sumerian civilization of the Middle East is now acknowledged, but the Sumerian peoples were lost in antiquity until the 1920's. The great Minoan civilization, the first truly European culture, was only uncovered in 1904 by Sir Arthur Evans. Both the Sumerians and the Minoans were literate, but we still have only a partial knowledge of their history.

In Asia, the powerful and sophisticated Indus civilization, contemporary with Egypt and Sumeria, is known only by its staggeringly complex material remains and a completely undeciphered system of writing. The very existence of these huge cities of the Indus river valley was entirely unknown until 1922.

Fortunately for our understanding of the American portion of our global heritage, more work has been done in the archaeology of the Western Hemisphere in the last fifty years than in any other area on earth. So much has been done, in fact, that publication of results has lagged far behind the work of the excavators. With each fresh discovery, each new excavation, the history of the great cultures of the Americas has been thrust ever farther back in time. Any summary, however generalized, may be overtaken tomorrow or next year. In brief, however, current findings give us this picture:

The American continents were peopled by nomadic hunters from Asia beginning at some time prior to 12,000 B.C. They crossed from Siberia into Alaska over a land or sea bridge probably in pursuit of the animals on which their livelihood depended. By 9,000 years ago the descendants of these first settlers of the Americas had reached the southern tip of South America.

The first discoverers and colonizers of the New World were among the world's most skilled hunters. It has even been suggested that the disappearance of some species of the fauna of North America (the mastodon, giant sloth, the American camel and horse) may have been due to the efficiency in the hunt of these first Americans.

There are great gaps in the archaeological record, which consists for the most part of the ashes of ancient campfires, stone and bone tools and projectile points, rope sandals, and a few partial skeletons of the hunters themselves. There is still much controversy over the dating of these relics and the nature of the men and women who made them.

A sufficient consensus exists, however, to indicate that by 4,000 B.C. American man had penetrated into almost every corner of the Western Hemisphere and in a few favoured areas had begun to develop a true civilization based on the cultivation of food plants. Of these the most important was maize, or, as the European explorers called it, "Indian corn." Present knowledge points to the central Mexican plateau as the place where primitive American farmers first learned to domesticate the wild ancestor of maize, teosinte.

Once a population finds a way to feed itself independently of the vagaries of the chase, permanent settlements become possible. In the Americas two kinds of permanent settlements began to appear in the third millenium before the birth of Christ. One type depended on the harvest of the sea, the other on the harvest of the land. In Middle America the development of villages, and hence of civilization, depended almost entirely on the latter. On the western coast of South America huge middens of sea shells mark the sites of villages anciently fed by the protein-rich waters of the Pacific currents. A site at Huaco Prieta on the Peruvian coast was settled as early as 2,500 B.C. One-roomed houses built of whalebone and timbers have been found near the enormous piles of mollusc shells and fish bones that represent the diet of these peoples.

By 2,000 B.C. there were flourishing villages and towns throughout the areas where the cultivation of maize and other food products had made sedentary living possible. Dzibilchaltún, a Mayan site north of Merida, capital of the state of Yucatan, was already a fair-sized settlement by 1,000 B.C.

The first true civilization to emerge was that of the people known to archaeology as the Olmecs ("the rubber people") of the Gulf of Mexico. By 900 B.C. the Olmecs were building large ceremonial centres at La Venta and Tres Zapotes in the states of Tabasco and Vera Cruz. At

La Venta one of the earliest and largest of the pyramids so characteristic of the ancient American cultures was built. It is not four-square; the sides have individual angles of slope. Its size – 420 feet long, 240 feet wide, and 110 feet high – bears silent testimony to the degree of community organization achieved by these people.

The Olmec civilization lasted for some 500 years – until about 400 B.C. – and left some of the most enigmatic remains ever encountered by archaeologists. Huge basalt heads as tall as a man and jade masks, both representing figures of negroid appearance; intricately designed mosaic floors carefully buried under earth as soon as they were completed; little jade figures of disturbingly non-human crying babies – all are said to have had something to do with a cult of a "were-jaguar" – a creature half man, half animal.

In architecture they were not as advanced as the peoples who followed them, but they seem to have been the inventors of the calendrical, numerical, and mathematical systems which later became common throughout Middle America. In this field they were far ahead of the peoples of the Old World at this time; their positional arithmetic makes a mockery of the clumsy Roman system. Their astronomical and mathematical genius entitles them to first rank among the civilized people of the world.

From its homeland in the swampy jungles of the Gulf Coast, the Olmec influence extended over an enormous area; throughout Mexico and Central America and even into South America. All the later civilizations of Middle America sprang from the Olmec cradle. By 300 B.C. the people we know as the Zapotecs, who lived on the Pacific coast in the narrow southern neck of Mexico, were making astronomical observations based on the Olmec system. At Monte Albán and Mitla in the state of Oaxaca there are carved figures resembling the exotic sculpture of La Venta and Tres Zapotes.

A century or so later the great Mayan civilization blossomed in full flower, its genesis marked by the building of great ceremonial centres in the Mexican states of Chiapas and Campeche and in neighbouring Guatemala and British Honduras. Architecturally, scientifically, and socially, the Maya outstripped all other native civilizations of the New World. Their calendar achieved an accuracy greater than that by which we mark the passage of time; their art and architecture equalled and in some respects exceeded the accomplishments of the ancient nations of the Old World.

Meanwhile in South America, a similar outburst of civilizing energy was taking place. The first clear indications of an emergence from a primitive state appear about 2,500 B.C. The coastal people were fishermen; inland, new food products were developed including the misnamed "Irish" potato. One of the greatest agricultural discoveries was that by which the poisonous manioca plant was treated so as to become a nourishing and easily preserved source of food (sago). Maize was also grown but not as successfully as in Central America until about 800 B.C. when traders from the ubiquitous Olmec peoples brought in an improved variety. At the same time the Olmec cult of the jaguar was introduced.

By the dawn of the Christian era there were cities and ceremonial centres in South America that were already several hundred years old. Huge structures – temples and pyramids – existed, requiring the coordinated workmanship of great numbers of people under a stable administration.

All these complex societies belonged in the category which European archaeology has named the Stone Age. There was some metallurgical knowledge in use among the civilizations of South America; for the rest, stone and bone tools provided the only mechanical means for the building of some of the largest stone structures on earth.

Because generations of Europeans have been raised on the idea that civilization and metallurgy are somehow synonymous, there has been a reluctance in many learned circles to grant the native American cultures the rank of "civilization." In Europe and Asia it came to be assumed in the last century that an age of stone tools, the "Stone Age," was followed by a Bronze Age and that by an Iron Age. This progression came to be the yardstick by which the rise of a people to a true civilization was measured. Even in the old lands, this arbitrary classification has not always worked out satisfactorily; in the New World it fails utterly to account for the heights of intellectual activity reached by the builders of the great astronomical observatory at Chichén Itzá in Yucatan, to cite but one example.

The minds of the natives of the Americas were cast in a different mould from that of their European brothers. The American minds were introspective, subtle, given to the consideration of the internal rather than the external aspects of their environment. Their thinking was oriental rather than occidental, which may, if one wishes, be ascribed to their Asiatic origin, possibly further influenced by later physical contacts from that same source. A religious or philosophical concept was much more likely to inflame their imaginations and spur their mental energies than a new method of erecting a pyramid.

A striking exemplification of this frame of mind is the Mayan preoccupation with mathematics, especially with the use of that science to record the passage of time. Their numerical system was one of the world's simplest, as well as one of the most advanced. A symbolic dot equalled one unit, a bar equalled five. The system was vigesimal – based on the number twenty. Numerical calculations were expressed by placement in vertical columns, each ascending position increasing in value by multiples of twenty from bottom to top. A third symbol represented the abstract concept of zero, without which all but the most simplified calculations are impossible. The Maya invented and applied these two principles – positional arithmetic and the use of zero – centuries before they were introduced into Europe by the Arabs.

It was, however, the purpose to which these discoveries were put that makes the Maya unique among the world's peoples. The earliest civilizations of the Old World used numbers principally to record commercial transactions – to which great stacks of clay invoices in many ancient sites in the Near East attest. The Maya, on the other hand, used their much more advanced numerical system to record the mysterious march of days. They were fascinated – some European scholars say "obsessed" – with the meaning of numbers and the nature of time.

I believe that it was precisely this mental climate upon which the Quetzalcoatl epic fed. I believe further that the various forms of the legend conceal an actual, historical person. The legends themselves strongly imply the historicity of their central figure. The prototypal Quetzalcoatl was treated initially not as a god but as a man – an alien who was at first accepted as teacher, priest, and guide and only later, long after his death, deified. I believe that a friendly spiritual environment enabled either the culture-hero himself or his transmitted teachings to invade successfully an area as large as Europe.

The nature of these teachings is also made clear in the legends. In every instance the hero is credited with bringing about great changes, most especially in the field of ethics and religious practices. If this was the case, one would then expect to find some factual, which is to say archaeological, proof of an historical event of the dimensions implied by the legend. One would also hope by this means to arrive at some approximate date for this event.

It has now become quite clear that some event of major historical importance did in fact occur in pre-Columbian America which led to a widespread revolution in religion and ethics, and that the beginning of this process may be dated with a good degree of accuracy to the first half of the second century after the birth of Christ.

In the chapter dealing with the Quetzalcoatl legend I have already cited the conclusions reached by the excavating teams at the site of Teotihuacán. Briefly summarized, they agree that the great city had been extensively rebuilt in the first half of the second century A.D. by newcomers to the area who were associated with the cult of Quetzalcoatl.

In South America archaeology has revealed a similar development. According to the legend, the culture-hero Bochica, white, bearded, and alien, is said to have revolutionized the way of life among those ancient people now known as Mochica who lived in present-day Colombia. Archaeology has revealed that such an event did occur, that the influence was intrusive, and that it probably happened in the second century of the Christian era. Hermann Leicht, writing in 1944, summarized his findings:

> There is absolutely no archaeological evidence to show that the later Chimu culture gradually grew on the spot from these first inhabitants. On the contrary, the most ancient art of the Chimu [Mochica] is easily distinguishable from the finds which can be attributed to the autochthonous population. In its first stage can already be seen quite clearly its connection with Central American culture .... There is no possible doubt that the ancestors of the Chimu [Mochica] in possession of a culture that had already evolved from the archaic stage, migrated here from the north in the second or third century of our calendar.[1]

The still-mysterious Tiahuanaco culture associated with the cult of Viracocha also represents an intrusive influence, and it, too, is dated to the second or third centuries of the Christian era. Of what happened here, let me again quote Hermann Leicht:

> Should we succeed in unravelling the hidden meaning of the fish

symbol and its related symbols, the question of the origin of the Tiahuanaco culture will one day be solved by the research spirit. We shall perhaps find that it was not a pure sun cult as is usually accepted today but that on those heights one of the most remarkable revolutions in religious history took place, namely the exciting but unexplained transition from moon to sun worship.[2]

At great remove geographically from the huge and enigmatic Gate of the Sun at Tiahuanaco, the enormous earthen mounds – erected by the tribes and peoples once known collectively as the Mound Builders – also bear witness to the spiritual awakening of the Americas at the dawn of the Christian era.

As classified by their surviving artifacts and structures, these mysterious builders are known as the Adena, Point Peninsula, and Hopewell people. The names identify the type-sites where their distinctive cultures were first recognized. Speaking generally, the Adena and Hopewell sites are found concentrated in the basins of the Ohio and Mississippi rivers. The home of the Point Peninsula people was New York State and southern Canada.

The structures erected by the Adena and Point Peninsula peoples were in the main what are called "effigy mounds" – representations of birds, animals, and snakes. The mounds are so large that the figures they represent are readily identifiable only from above, from the air, by the gods. The Great Serpent Mound in Adams County, Ohio, for instance, is 1,330 feet long with an average height of three feet. The mound at Peterborough, Ontario, is in the middle range in size – 189 feet in length, an average of five feet in height and twenty-four feet in width. Here, as in many Adena and Point Peninsula sites, the mound served as a memorial for unknown tribal leaders. In the head were found four cremation burials to which, by radioactive Carbon 14 analysis, a date of approximately 130 A.D. has been assigned.

At a much later period the Hopewell people began building a different kind of mound – rudimentary pyramids, somewhat after the Mexican style. Like the effigy mounds, they were built on an heroic scale. The best known is the great mound at Cahokia on the Mississippi river near East St. Louis, Illinois. It is a flattened pyramid more than 100 feet high, 1,080 feet long, and 710 feet wide. It is the centre of a complex of more than 400 smaller, flat-topped mounds.

Still later and farther south, in the lower reaches of the Mississippi valley, another culture group, almost certainly immigrants from Mexico, began building mounds in the true Middle-American pattern. Popularly they are known as the "Temple Mound builders."

An academic controversy has raged for many years around the chronology of the Adena and Hopewell peoples. First one and then the other has been assigned priority. The latest evidence seems to indicate that in at least some areas the two cultures existed coevally. There is no doubt, however, that the burial mounds preceded the temple mounds, the first appearing in the opening centuries of the Christian era, the latter nearly a thousand years later. Both were undeniably religious in nature.

All these cultures – Adena, Point Peninsula, Hopewell, and the Temple Mound people – represent explosive outbursts of cultural energy directed into religious channels, one arising in the second or third centuries A.D., a second nearly a millenium later – precisely the pattern observed in Middle and South America.

There is more.

The older artifacts found in burial sites built before 500 A.D. – carved stone pipes and other sculptures – portray individuals differing in human type from those representations found in the later temple mound period. The latter represent persons possessing definite Indian characteristics, strongly resembling Mexican images of the same period. Anthropologically speaking, the earlier peoples tended to be brachycephalic (round-headed); the later, dolichocephalic (long-headed). Of the distribution of these two types I quote from a standard anthropology text:

> Most series of premodern skulls, that is to say, of individuals who died before the last ten thousand years, are on the average dolichocephalic. Most Negroid populations of today are dolichocephalic; so too are most northern and southern European populations and the American Indians of coastal districts. An east-west belt of peoples across Europe ranges from mesocephalic to extremely brachycephalic; as do also some Indians of the interior districts of the United States.[3]

We see, then, in the Ohio and Mississippi river valleys in the first 500 years of the Christian era, a group of round-headed people introducing to the generally long-headed native population a theocratic society centred on great man-made mounds celebrating the greatest mystery in human life – death.

That the society introduced was theocratic is borne out by the conclusions reached in James B. Griffin's monumental work, *Archeology of the Eastern United States*:

> It can certainly be said that the development of the earthwork pattern is along ceremonial lines devoted to the religious concepts and beliefs of the group and that this was probably dominated by male shamans who were promulgating the interpretation of the relationship of man to the universe for the population as a whole. This suggests the development of a specialized priesthood.

To sum up this very brief survey, the evidence now available shows that there was a great explosion of cultural energy in the Americas beginning in the early part of the second century A.D. Its effects extended from the mid-western United States to the *altiplano* of Peru. It is represented by massive structures requiring the cooperative and organized work of thousands of people.

The driving force behind these efforts was, without exception, religious. In every instance cited in this chapter, it was an abrupt transition from one cult to another. In the sense that older religious systems were overthrown or overlaid by a fresher and more vigorous set of beliefs, it can be termed a religious revolution comparable in its far-reaching effects on the native peoples of the Americas to the introduction, by fiat, of Christianity by Constantine the Great in the fourth century or the Protestant Reformation in the sixteenth.

In each case the archaeological evidence shows that the new influence was intrusive. There was no time for the slow development postulated by Vaillant and others. It appeared suddenly, as a fully developed religious system with a strong trend towards monotheism. It absorbed or diverted to its own uses earlier, polytheistic practices, much in the fashion of early European (Gentile) Christianity. Significantly, it apparently did not affect the technological development of the peoples it touched. There is no abrupt transition in pottery styles or building techniques, for instance. These material evidences of already-established civilizations were simply put to a new purpose – the glorification of a new faith. This was an intellectual and religious revolution, not an economic or political one.

All the literate or proto-literate native nations affected have left legendary accounts of the apostles of the new belief. In every instance these men are described as differing from the native populations; frequently they are carefully described as white, bearded, and wearing long, flowing robes. These accounts, whether from the highlands of Mexico or the great plateau on which sits Lake Titicaca in Peru, preserve a remarkable unanimity of expression. The leader of the newcomers always resembled, in all important aspects, the prototypal hero, Quetzalcoatl.

We must now consider the material evidence for the physical appearance of these newcomers.

Chapter Eight

THE BEARDED FACES

It is fairly simple to register any figure with a beard under the heading Xiuhtecutli or Huehueteotl, the Nahuatl name for the "fire" or "old" god. Utilizing this tempting device further, one can forget that the real question is not so much whether a figure does or does not represent a "fire god," but to explain the presence of a beard (which real Indians do not have) as a symbol of this deity and why most representations of this kind show decidedly Semitic characteristics.

— Alexander von Wuthenau, *Pre-Columbian Terracottas.*

1

We started out with a collection of legends dealing with the epic adventures of a group of white, bearded strangers, said to have been responsible for introducing a new religion to the peoples of pre-Columbian America. Supporting evidence from archaeology proves that there was indeed a great spiritual awakening throughout the hemisphere beginning in the second century of the Christian era and that this influence, wherever felt, came from outside the communities affected. Further, it has been demonstrated that this awakening was not the result of a slow, tortuous progress by a native people struggling to understand the secrets of the universe, but rather a dramatically sudden event of unknown origin.

Who were the agents of this new cult? Were they natives of the Americas, emerging from some intellectual and spiritual heart-land as yet undiscovered by the archaeologists?

The legends say they were white, like the Europeans, had beards, and wore long, flowing robes.

Is there any tangible proof of such statements?

Almost from the beginning of the European settlement of these continents, artifacts have been found depicting bearded figures of non-Indian appearance. However, only in recent years has any real attempt been made to correlate this evidence.

The first serious study of these unusual artifacts was made by

74

George C. Vaillant. He was prompted to his research by an odd baked clay figurine which had turned up in the Rio Balsas region on the border between the Mexican states of Michoacan and Guerrero. The little figure, three and a quarter inches in diameter, represented the head of a man with protruding eyes and ears, a malevolently grinning mouth and a large curly beard terminating in two points.

As Vaillant remarked in "A Bearded Mystery," an article in *Natural History*, the features were "most unlike those of the various American Indian physical types." In his speculations as to its origin he ranged widely, to Europe, Asia and Africa, finding the closest parallel to the type in the Middle East, especially Mesopotamia.

Since Vaillant's article appeared in 1931, many such finds have been reported, discussed and illustrated. Surprisingly, however, little or no effort was made to classify these bearded images as to type, locale, and chronology until the publication in 1965 by Alexander von Wuthenau of a study of pre-Columbian clay images. In his introduction to the English translation, published in 1970,[1] von Wuthenau points out what every student of Middle American history has discovered – that the soil of Mexico is sown with literally millions of little terracotta images of human beings. (The private collection of the late Diego Rivera, the great Mexican muralist, contained no less than 60,000 such pieces.) The greater part of this enormous mass of portraits in clay, especially those belonging to the later periods, was mass-produced – cast from moulds. There remains, however, a great number of works produced, individually, by artists of outstanding merit.

Von Wuthenau was the first scholar to study these little artifacts carefully with a view to classifying them in the ways I suggested above. He came to some striking conclusions:

> One of the most startling things they reveal is an awareness and even an intimate acquaintance on the artist's part with the main characteristics of *all the races of mankind*.

His second conclusion is even more astonishing:

> Archaeologically and historically it is of the utmost significance that these characteristics appeared at very early times in the art of the New World.

In summation, von Wuthenau discovered that among the terracottas of the late pre-Classic and early Classic periods (which together cover, approximately, the years from 600 B.C. to 600 A.D.) by far the commonest types represented persons of markedly non-Indian characteristics. At the same time von Wuthenau gives no indication that he considers the *artists* to have been non-Indian. In other words, at the dawn of the Classic period of the Middle American civilizations, native artists were engaged in turning out by the thousands images of persons who were totally unlike themselves.

Among the hundreds of thousands of such artifacts that passed through his hands, von Wuthenau found clearly recognizable representations of Asiatics, Europeans, and Africans. The rarest type was that showing Negroid characteristics; next rarest were the Asiatics. Of the white type, says von Wuthenau, there are so many examples "no one can remain unaware of them!" Among these latter, those bearing recognizably Semitic features are the most numerous of all.

Hundreds of them have beards.

When von Wuthenau first brought his discoveries to the attention of specialists in the field of Middle American archaeology at the International Congress of Americanists in Barcelona in 1964, he was told that his carefully garnered examples merely represented "stylizations" made by the Indian artists. The argument is altogether too specious.

2

Even before Alexander von Wuthenau dropped his bombshell, discoveries of portraits in clay, stone, and other materials had already pointed the way to the same inevitable conclusion. Each succeeding discovery caused a reaction ranging from a few academic ripples to popular tidal waves, depending on the public relations skills of the discoverers.

Of the bearded images that have reached the stage of publication in one form or another, I have discerned four major types. Two of these represent persons with markedly non-Indian features. One of the two shows a thin-faced man with a well-groomed, pointed beard. The other is that of a heavy-set, square-faced man with a full, rounded beard. In this connection it is interesting to note that there are conflicting versions of the Quetzalcoatl legend, one of which refers to the hero's hair and beard as being fair – "yellow as the straw" – while the other describes him as a large man, broad-browed, with huge eyes, long black hair and a great rounded beard – "*la barba grande y redonda*", as Juan

76

de Torquemada puts it. The beard on the Rio Balsas figure was painted black.

The third type of bearded image represents faces of the familiar Amerindian variety. In such cases the beard is often obviously false; in some instances lines are clearly visible showing the attachment by which the beard was suspended from the ears. It need hardly be pointed out that we have here an imitation of a revered prototype, in the fashion of the artificial beards shown on representations of the Egyptian pharaohs.[2]

There are a few examples of what may be called a fourth type. Here, the chins of persons of identifiable Indian origin are graced with a few straggly hairs which can scarcely be called beards by European standards. It is reported that Moctezuma, emperor of the Aztecs, wore such a beard in imitation of the great hero-god Quetzalcoatl.

The distribution of the bearded images roughly approximates the area influenced by what I have called the "spiritual awakening" of the Americas – that is, Middle and South America. The establishment of a chronology is extremely difficult since few of these images have actually been found *in situ* by qualified archaeologists. Of those that have been adequately documented, one of the most striking is the tiny jade "idol" found in a sarcophagus inside the Temple of the Inscriptions at Palenque by Alberto Ruz Lhuillier in 1949. Since Señor Ruz' sensational discovery of an intact Mayan tomb has been lavishly reported in both the popular press and the learned periodicals, and since there can be no question as to the authenticity of his research, we may use his "jade idol" and its setting for a more detailed examination of the nature of the bearded images with non-Indian features.

From the time Alberto Ruz Lhuillier found a movable slab in the floor of the little temple crowning the pyramid at Palenque until he raised the lid of the coffin seventy feet below, four years elapsed – years of painstaking, back-breaking work which include the clearing of two carefully constructed and carefully blocked flights of stairs. The great sarcophagus was carved out of stone with a flared and flattened base strongly reminiscent of Egyptian mummy-cases. It contained the skeleton of a man of well-above-average height for Mayan males; in life he probably stood about five feet eight inches. Although he was obviously a person of great importance, his teeth were normal, not inset with ornaments or filed, as was usual for adult Maya of high rank. Calendrical glyphs found in the burial chamber recorded dates corresponding to 603 A.D. and 633 A.D.

Near the skeleton was the little piece of jade, beautifully carved, representing a bearded male figure, hands clasped across the chest. The beard is trimmed to a neat point; the eyes and nose are large and the head is crowned with a strange cap with something like a tassel on top. The overall effect is Semitic.

The little idol seldom gets more than a few words of notice in reports of the spectacular find but those few words are, for our purposes here, significant. The archaeologists identify it as an image of Kinich Ahau, the Mayan sun god. But Kinich Ahau, Lord of the Eye of the Sun, is identified with Itzamna, the Mayan hero-god, whom I have equated with Quetzalcoatl of Teotihuacán.

The idol and the tomb in which it was found are useful to us in other ways as well. Legend tells us that Palenque was founded by the hero Votan, and in his city is found a great pyramid erected to contain the bones of a very important person – in all probability a priest-king who was buried holding in his hand an image of one who may have been his great predecessor in the high priesthood of Palenque, Votan himself.

Because the image was found by a trained archaeologist in a specific setting which can be at least approximately dated, it serves as a useful "proof text," as it were, to other, similar images of uncertain provenance and unknown dates. The profile of the image, with its pointed beard, large eyes and prominent nose, has many echoes – on a clay rattle found in Guatemala; on the back of a slate mirror from southeastern Vera Cruz; in a pottery head found at Tres Zapotes in 1940, and on a brazier representing the god of fire Huehueteotl (an aspect of Quetzalcoatl in the Aztec pantheon), among others. In some instances the likenesses between these figures extend to the headgear. There is a strong resemblance, which can scarcely be accidental, between the tasseled cap worn by the Palenque figure and the conical head-dress worn by the "suave, Mephistophelian" figure from Tres Zapotes. Nor can any of these images be considered formalized abstractions. Of the Tres Zapotes head, Matthew W. Stirling, its discoverer, said: "Because of its life-like appearance, it is probably a study of a prominent person." The others have the same life-like quality and are obviously portraits. They are not copies, one of another. They are individual in style, reflecting the separate artists' impressions of their subject.

I believe that their subject is the same, in each case. The similarities are too great for them to be portraits of different men. What differences there are, can easily be interpreted as reflecting various stages in the age of the subject. The head on the Vera Cruz mirror is that of a young man. The pottery head from Tres Zapotes shows a mature individual. The Palenque idol represents a man in possibly late middle age. The brazier-bearing Huehueteotl is an old man. Huehueteotl, the fire god, was also called the "old god" by the Aztecs. I believe that the adjective was used by them in two senses – referring to the apparent age of the figure and the antiquity of his worship. The Aztecs were newcomers to the Valley of Mexico. Quetzalcoatl had lived and died nearly 1,000 years before the Nahuatl conquerors had arrived. There are in the Aztecan pantheon two other gods – more than likely ancestral dieties – whom they seem to have equated with Huehueteotl.

Finally, it is worth noting that the Mayan glyph standing for Itzamna – who according to tradition died in Izamal – shows us, in profile, the head of a very old man with but a single tooth, cut to a point, in his upper jaw, still with the little pointed beard.

The second of the two figures – the square-faced man with the large, rounded beard – is not nearly as commonly found nor is there any indication of a protracted life span. The two images which I have seen of this personage show him in virile maturity. Both are in the great Museo Nacional de Antropologia in Mexico City. The better-known one is popularly called "The Wrestler" and is credited to the Olmec culture. The second is in the museum's Mayan collection and is recognizably an image of the same person, although the position of the arms is different.

There are many other examples of bearded images which could be cited – for instance the so-called "Uncle Sam" figure at the base of a basalt stele found at La Venta, in the State of Tabasco, Olmec country. Another is the strange little figure from the area of the Totonacs, another Gulf Coast people. The figure wears something roughly resembling a Roman helmet, his beard represented by striated lines in the clay of the cheeks and chin.

The examples I have chosen to highlight in this chapter are all from Mexico and Central America. They are among the best known and are especially remarkable for their naturalism. Literally hundreds of such figures have been found throughout those areas of Mexico, and Central and South America wherever the legend of the hero-god was current. The great majority of them, however, are stylized, formalized abstractions possibly taken from earlier models.

The British writer, Geoffrey Ashe,[3] pointed out in 1962 that the naturalistic portrait images so far reported tend to be concentrated in a nuclear area extending roughly from the site of Tajin to the La Venta site of the Gulf Coast of Mexico and inland as far as Teotihuacán and perhaps to the State of Guerrero (where the Rio Balsas figure was found). Outside this area, Mr. Ashe argued, the bearded images tend to be highly stylized, copies of copies. As to the chronology of these portrait faces, Mr. Ashe has arrived at a dating for them which agrees quite closely with that established by many researchers – the last pre-Christian century or the first of the Christian era.

Mr. Ashe's conclusions are well thought out. It is true that as one moves out of the nuclear area the bearded images tend to be much less realistic. In many of the South American examples, for instance, the layman will have problems recognizing the crude facial markings as being beards at all. The examples from the ancient site of Tiahuanaco which Thor Heyerdahl illustrated in his *American Indians in the Pacific* would, I am sure, baffle even that scholarly gentleman were it not for the realistic tradition from Mexico and Central America which makes it possible for us to identify the knobs, scratches, and vague markings on the chins of these images as beards and not chokers or necklaces.

I do, however, feel that Mr. Ashe, in his shrewd and timely stylistic analysis, may have overlooked one important point – the artistic skills of the native artists in the various areas under consideration.

From a very early time the peoples of Middle America had shown a high degree of skill in the portrayal of character. In the millenium or more before the birth of Christ, literally hundreds of thousands of little clay figurines were made, often identified as fertility images, which are still being found at all of the ancient sites. Anyone who has had the privilege of seeing a collection of these has been delighted at the facility the ancient artists showed in the delineation of character and emotion. The same tradition does not hold to nearly the same degree in South America, with the outstanding exception of the artists of the Mochica (or Early Chimu) culture.

Is it not possible that where the bearded images lack the naturalism of the clay head found at Tres Zapotes for instance, we are dealing not with a deliberate stylization or a copy of a copy, but merely with less skilled artists? In many ways I find this an easier theory to accept than Mr. Ashe's dissemination of copies. A single instance may suffice to illustrate my point. In Northern Peru many portrait pottery jars are found somewhat reminiscent of the English Toby jugs of the eighteenth century. One of the figures represented is that of a seated man with large eyes, a prominent nose and a pointed beard which is sometimes painted white. He wears a peculiar flat turban which sometimes has ears or horns. He is usually portrayed wearing large ear plugs. These images bear a startling resemblance to the little jade figurine found by Señor Alberto Ruz Lhuillier in the Temple of the Inscriptions at Palenque. There are the same large eyes and prominent nose, the same kind of moustache and beard. The pointed cap of the Palenque figure has been replaced by a turban. The Palenque image has no ear plugs. In all other respects the figures are identical in pose and features.

If we accept Mr. Ashe's stylistic theory, we will have to assume a remarkably widespread distribution of copies of the Palenque "idol" at a time, incidentally, when we have no evidence of extensive trade or travel between the two areas. It is asking a little too much to assume that a single copy spawned all of the images. It is considerably simpler and, I think, more logical, to assume that the Mochica jars merely represent the work of less skilled artists or of artists with a different style. Many other subjects have been represented on these jars with a degree of realism that has led to them being termed "portraits" – that is to say, they portrayed living persons known to the artists. I see no reason why we should come to any different conclusion with respect to the bearded images.

3

If the naturalistic sculptures found in Middle and South America were portraits of living persons known to the artists, who were the models?

They were certainly not American Indians. At least they belonged to no native tribe or culture of which we have any anthropological or archaeological evidence to this date. Their appearance strongly suggests that they were aliens to the communities which they visited – a fact borne out both by the hero-legends and by the archaeological evidence.

This is the greatest mystery of pre-Columbian times. It has suffered from no lack of explication, ranging from the scholarly to the fantastic, as Dr. Robert Wauchope, director of the Middle American Research Institute at Tulane University, New Orleans, has acidly pointed out in his amusing little book, *Lost Tribes and Sunken Continents*.

Dr. Wauchope's book also illustrates the extreme reluctance on the part of the academic world to entertain the notion of any kind of contact between the Americas and the other continents prior to the voyages of the Vikings in the eleventh century. Indeed, until the excavation of an indisputably Norse settlement at L'Anse au Meadows, Newfoundland, in the 1960's, academics were unwilling to accept the historicity of the Norse sagas which told of the voyages to Vinland. With each new discovery this position is being slowly and inexorably eroded, sometimes to the embarrassment and confusion of the specialists. Cottie Burland, an English writer who has written extensively on American antiquities, has perhaps unconsciously revealed his perplexity on this subject in a recent popular account, *The People of the Ancient Americas*. On page 48, he says, in reference to the appearance of beards on some sculptures from Mexico:

> Since beards occur, although only rarely, among American Indians, there is no reason for postulating any contact with bearded people from the Old World.

Earlier, on page 46, with reference to a beard on a Zapotec monument, he says:

> Whether the beard has significance is unknown, but it should be noted that some American Indians naturally grow small beards and this does not necessarily indicate any foreign connections.

On page 55 in the description of a bearded figure, sculptured with obvious realism on a stele at Tepatlazco, Vera Cruz, Dr. Burland has apparently changed his mind:

> Both figures wear beards. That on the ball player may be a false one to represent a star god, but the official appears to wear both beard and natural moustache. It is to be noted that most of the bearded figures in older Mexican art are found in Olmec and Totonac material, near the Gulf Coast. They may represent some tradition, or

82

even a physical inheritance from a few drift voyagers from the old world.

Many scholars have now moved to a flexible position, acknowledging that the slowly accumulating mass of evidence implies some kind of contact with the Americas but refusing to speculate on its nature.

If the prototypal Quetzalcoatl and his companions were not natives of the Americas, where did they come from? Africa? Asia? Europe?

According to Alexander von Wuthenau, newcomers came from all three continents in the nuclear period of Mexican civilization. I am prepared to accept this. But where did *Quetzalcoatl* come from?

Africa? A crossing of the South Atlantic from the west coast of Africa to the coast of the Gulf of Mexico, utilizing the South Equatorial Current, is a much simpler feat than the crossing of the North Atlantic Ocean. The proposition is quite tenable, therefore, providing one can postulate at the same time a West African population sufficiently advanced in civilization to make such a planned or accidental voyage. As it happens, the South Equatorial Current is born off precisely that portion of the African continent that produced the highest ancient black culture, the crowning artistic achicvements of which are the Benin bronzes.

I suggest therefore that a cultural contact between West Africa and the Gulf of Mexico is not only possible but probable and that it took place sometime during the first millenium before the birth of Christ and was either wholly or partially responsible for the burgeoning of the oldest-known Middle American civilization, the Olmec.

Some writers have guessed that the thick-lipped individuals so often shown in Olmec portraiture, both in terracotta and monolithic statuary, were black slaves brought on a hypothetical voyage by the ubiquitous Phoenicians. The slave theory is seriously damaged by Professor von Wuthenau's claim that the Negroid types usually represent persons of high caste in the social order:

> It is precisely the Negroid representations which often indicate personalities of high position, who can unhesitatingly be compared to the outstanding Negroes who served as models for great works of art in Egypt and in Nigeria.[4]

The most generally accepted "official" theory is that the Olmec figurines and sculptures which occur throughout a wide area of Middle

America, represent not Negroes but a sort of totem "were-jaguar" – a creature half man-child, half jaguar. Many stylistic features strengthen this interpretation but I believe that we are dealing here again with an attempt on the part of a native population to "marry" an earlier, barbarian tradition incorporating a tribal jaguar totem with the strange features of the leaders of a more sophisticated alien culture.

To sum up: Africa is acceptable as a source of one of the influences shaping the development of the civilization of the Americas. However, Africa must be ruled out as the source both of Quetzalcoatl and the religious beliefs he instituted. The hero was not black. His features are not Negroid, nor does the faith he taught have any parallels among the religious practices of West Africa in the period under review.

What about von Wuthenau's "Asiatics"? Of late years a number of scholars, including such men as Dr. Gordon F. Ekholm and the ethnologist, Dr. Robert Heine-Geldern, have claimed to find many cultural features in Middle America which point to the possibility of a contact with Southeast Asia at a time – 100 A.D. to 600 A.D. – of vigorous Indian colonial expansion. Some of the parallels cited, particularly an involved use of a lotus motif in both areas, are very striking and have won many converts to the theory of a transPacific contact either preceding or shortly after the beginning of the Christian era.[5] Dr. Heine-Geldern's theory has been much strengthened by the discovery of a localized pottery technique at a South American site whose only known parallel is the Jomon pottery of Japan dating to more than a millennium before the birth of Christ. While conservative archaeologists are still disputing the ancient Japanese influence, the later Southeast Asian contact is being fairly widely accepted, increasingly so as the realization dawns on the scientific community that mankind, even in prehistoric times, was vastly more mobile than was previously believed.

I see no good reason to reject Dr. Heine-Geldern's theory. I think it more than possible that transPacific travellers did on more than one occasion touch on the shores of Middle America and may even have returned to home base. There is some botanical evidence that the civilizing American food plant maize was exported from the Americas to Asia, quite possibly as the result of such a cultural contact.

However, I cannot accept Southeast Asia as the place of origin of Quetzalcoatl nor as the cradle of the revolution in religious ideas coincident with his appearance, for a number of reasons. In the first place, the various versions of the legend in Middle America consistently state that the hero came over the seas from the east. In South America he is said to have come from the north which is entirely logical if his first landfall was the Gulf of Mexico. Secondly, the bearded images bear no resemblance whatever to any known Asiatic people of the second century A.D. Thirdly, no artifacts of Asiatic origin have been assigned to the period of the "great awakening" – 100 to 200 A.D. Finally, and most importantly, the religious influence said to have been introduced by Quetzalcoatl and his comrades has no parallel in Southeast Asia, or in fact in any part of Asia in the second century A.D. Nothing in the religious practices and beliefs which first appeared in the Americas in that century shows any trace of the beliefs current in Asia at that time – no Buddhistic philosophies, no Indian, Japanese, or Chinese polytheism.[6]

On the other hand, all the evidence – archaeological, legendary, and religious – points strongly to a European rather than an Asiatic or African origin.

Between theory and provable fact there exists a great gulf. The bridge over this particular gulf is slowly being built. The discovery of at least two artifacts of European origin in Mexico has helped immeasurably.

Chapter Nine

THE MAN OF CALIXTLAHUACA

It is possible that ships from the west might have been blown into the Caribbean from the time, probably in the eighteenth century B.C. , when Cretan boats first entered the Atlantic. Certainly two Roman clay heads have been found in Mexico in a sound archaeological context.

— Cottie Burland, *The People of the Ancient Americas.*

The archaeological site of Calixtlahuaca lies in a mountain valley near Toluca, the capital of the State of Mexico. It is about forty miles west of Mexico City. Its altitude, 9,517 feet, makes it the highest-placed ancient site in the country. It is now a rather desolate looking, treeless place. Near a large lagoon stands a circular temple sacred to Quetzalcoatl in his guise as Ehecatl, the Lord of the Winds. It is an old site, having been occupied continuously for perhaps 2,000 years. Pottery sequences and other evidence show four different main influences at work over that span. The first residents were people belonging to the archaic period of Mexican history. They probably settled on the site about 500 B.C. In succession the inhabitants came under the influence of the culture of Teotihuacán and then by that of the Toltecs of Tula. Finally the city was captured by the Aztecs under their emperor Ahuitzotl in 1476 and destroyed by them in 1502.

The temple of Quetzalcoatl apparently belongs to the second of the four periods in the history of Calixtlahuaca. As nearly as can be determined the building of the structure was begun about 500 A.D., when Teotihuacán was still exerting a powerful influence on the thought and civilization of most of Mexico and Central America.

Round temples and pyramids are not common in Middle America. Where they occur they are invariably associated with the cult of Quetzalcoatl. The symbolism of the form is said to represent the ability of the god, as master of the winds, to pass where he will, unimpeded by the subtended angles of walls or the corners of the world. In a later period when an astronomical cult superseded or overlaid the cult of Quetzalcoatl, such round structures were more often used as observatories, as in the case of the Caracol at Chichén Itzá.

Towards the end of the year 1933, a well-known Mexican archaeologist, José García Payón, was conducting excavations at Calixtlahuaca, which site includes in addition to the temple other buildings of great interest, especially the *calmecac* portion of the site – the residences and schools belonging to the religious sect responsible for the worship at the temple. In the course of his work Dr. García discovered a platform which presented that kind of occupation stratification so justly beloved by archaeologists. There were three levels of use, each well separated from the others, the top layer representing the most recent occupation of the site, the bottom the oldest. Separating this bottom layer from the occupation debris of the second period above it was a sealed, undisturbed floor of native cement.

Under this floor Dr. García discovered a cremation burial. The person whose ashes were laid there was obviously of some importance. Among the "grave goods" were articles of gold, turquoise, copper, and rock crystal, in addition to clay seals and various items of pottery. All these were items of a type often found in such burials. Among them, however, was a totally unexpected find – a little clay head of strange appearance. It represented a person of markedly non-Indian features. Furthermore, it did not appear to be of Indian manufacture.

Dr. García duly recorded his find on pages 341 and 342 of the second volume of his notes on the excavations being conducted by him in the Tecaxic-Calixtlahuaca archaeological zone, noting that the little head was 2.5 centimeters in diameter. These notes, to my knowledge, have not yet been published.

In an article which appeared in the September-October 1960 issue of the *Bulletin of the Institute Nacional de Antropologia e Historia* of Mexico, Dr. García stated that he retained the head in his possession for many years as "una curiosidad." It may seem strange to many that so extraordinary a discovery should be viewed by its finder as a mere "curiosity." In defence of Dr. García's position it should be pointed out that any public announcement of such a find in 1933 – or indeed until very recently – would have brought down upon his head the scorn of his colleagues and the avid and unpleasant interest of scores of persons anxious to prove off-beat theories.

For reasons which must remain incomprehensible to the general reader, there has been a great reluctance on the part of most professional and conservative archaeologists to admit any remote possibility of a contact between the Old World and the New prior to the advent of Columbus. I truly believe that some of them would dispute this last fact, if they could find any grounds whatever for so doing.

I find it ironic that Dr. Gordon F. Ekholm, one of the architects of the theory of a transPacific contact between Southeast Asia and Middle America, should range himself with the opponents of a similar – but vastly easier – transatlantic contact. In a review article appearing in the September 25, 1971 issue of *The Saturday Review* he questions the identification of Dr. García's little clay head. That identification was made by his colleague and co-author of the transPacific contact theory, Dr. Robert Heine-Geldern.

In 1959, during a visit to Mexico, Dr. Heine-Geldern was shown the clay head and had a photograph made of it. The head itself was taken to the XIXth International Congress of Americanists held in Vienna in July 1960, by Dr. Ignacio Bernal, director of the National Museum of Anthropology of Mexico. There it was carefully examined by Dr. Heine-Geldern and other specialists who pronounced it genuine and of a type common in the Roman world in the second century A.D. A report on it was presented to the Congress, when it is said to have created a sensation.

Sensation or no, the presentation and identification of the little clay head received only a brief one-paragraph statement in the records of the Congress. In spite of the fact that the object was found by a respected archaeologist in the course of a dig carried out under strict scientific disciplines, such an authority as Gordon Ekholm could still, in 1971, refer to it as "a figurine head *supposedly* found in an *Aztec* grave in Mexico" (italics mine).

In further correspondence with Dr. García, Robert Heine-Geldern pointed out that the discovery was not unique. Professor Boehringer, of the German Archaeological Institute, was the authority for the statement that a little head of the same style had been seen in the Chicago museum; and Professor Walter Krickeberg, of Berlin, wrote that in 1888 Eduard Seler, the great German scholar, had reported the discovery of a Roman statuette of the goddess Venus in the Huaxtec region on the Gulf Coast. Unfortunately neither of these finds was well documented. Lacking documentation they cannot be seriously considered in the context of a putative transatlantic contact between the two shores of the Ocean Sea.

However, a find made near Queretaro, 134 miles northwest of Mexico City, of a clay head similar to that discovered by Dr. García, does not apparently suffer from this handicap. It was reported, with illustration, in the *Bulletin of the Institute Nacional de Antropologia e Historia* for September-October 1960. It was then said to be in the possession of Victor Blanco Labra, of the National University of Mexico.

Thus it would appear that two artifacts of European origin and probably Roman manufacture, dating from early in the Christian era, have been found, as Cottie Burland says, "in a sound archaeological context." In addition, there are unsubstantiated hints of further discoveries of like nature. The discovery and identification of these two figurines has lent weight to the theory of a transatlantic contact as early as the second century. The identifications have not gone unchallenged, but the challenges have been general rather than specific. For example, the art specialist, von Wuthenau, is told by technologists with little knowledge of art or style that his little Semitic heads are mere "Indian stylizations." The implication – that the Indian artists were able, in hundreds of cases, *accidentally* to portray physical types quite unlike themselves – simply will not do. Again, the strange discovery made by José García Payón at Calixtlahuaca is contemptuously dismissed by Dr. Gordon F. Ekholm. Dr. Ekholm not only casts doubt on Dr. García's technical competence – "a figurine head supposedly found" (see page 88) – but also commits an unforgivable solecism by attributing the grave in which the image was found to the Aztec civilization, which flourished more than a thousand years after the date reliably assigned to the inhumation. But then, as Dr. Ekholm himself has said, "there is clearly a strong bias against all attempts to prove transoceanic contacts or influences."

A theory to account for these discoveries could possibly be advanced – and for all I know may already have been advanced – that the figurines in question may have been borne across the Atlantic by dead men. The possibility of "drift voyages" at a very early time is now generally conceded by all but the most intransigently conservative observers. That being so, the question of the survival of the crew and passengers of such a vessel becomes a matter for consideration.

If we assume that a lost ship with a dead crew was finally washed ashore on the coast of the Gulf of Mexico by the vagaries of wind and current and that the vessel contained in its cargo a figurine head or two – or four – would this alone account for the growth of the legend of a fair, bearded stranger teaching a new religion? Would it account for the appearance in that coastal region of portrait heads of native manu-facture of living, non-Indian types?

I submit that such a theory will not for an instant hold water. These relics of Roman civilization were brought to the shores of the New World by living men, carrying a new faith.

Chapter Ten

TOYS AND ARCHES

My chariots rolled!

— Désiré Charnay, *Les anciennes villes.*

Any mention of the possibility of a contact between Europe and the Americas prior to 1000 A.D. elicits in many circles a conditioned response which hardly ever varies. "Why," these critics will ask, "is there then no evidence of the introduction of the principle of the wheel, advanced metallurgy, and the use of the keystone arch?"

The simplest counter-argument that I can advance is this: The crew of a vessel making an unpremeditated and accidental voyage of the kind that I have postulated would not necessarily have included a complement of blacksmiths, whitesmiths, architects, and masons. Any such voyage would almost certainly have been unplanned. The crew and passengers were not by intention colonists. They were not prepared to establish a settlement. The presence of any specialists aboard would have been purely fortuitous.

While any company of voyagers coming from the Mediterranean area would have been familiar with structures built employing the principle of the keystone arch, this does not automatically imply that all such travellers or any of them could actually construct such a building. The craft of the mason was a closely guarded secret down into the Middle Ages. By the same token it is highly unlikely that a random group of twentieth-century travellers cast upon a neolithic shore would be able to construct a modern, reinforced concrete building, no matter how many they had seen.

Furthermore, human societies tend to be conservative. The people of the Americas had developed building techniques of their own over a long period of time. Those techniques had proved suitable to their needs. Using them, they had been building monumental structures for at least half a millenium. Why should they abandon those principles at the whim of a handful of aliens who, on the evidence, seemed much more intent on converting souls than architecture?

I think it possible that many of those who advance such criticisms may have, uncritically, accepted those late accretions to the legend that credit the culture-hero not only with the establishment of a new religion, but with the very foundations of pre-Columbian American civilization.

What has been said about architecture applies equally to metallurgy. While a blacksmith would be a much more likely crew member on such a voyage than an architect or mason, he would have been gravely handicapped by the lack of raw materials. There do not seem to have been any free iron deposits known to the autochthonous population. Copper, silver, and gold were known and apparently first worked in Peru and Ecuador from which places the craft spread north into Middle America. Sophisticated techniques were employed including the *cire-perdue* or lost-wax method of casting. The Iron Age did not come to the Americas until the arrival of the Spaniards, nor is there any rational cause to demand its earlier introduction as a proof of transatlantic contact. In passing, it may be noted that the Viking settlement at L'Anse au Meadows in Newfoundland had iron weapons in the eleventh century, but there is no indication whatever of the craft having been passed on to the natives of that region.

To say that the *principle* of the wheel was unknown in the Americas is ridiculous and totally unwarranted. The moving of large masses of stone in the construction of pyramids, temples, and roads was obviously made possible only by the use of log rollers. The instant such a device is used, the principle of the use of the wheel is demonstrated. What such critics actually mean, of course, is that the principle of the wheel as adapted to wheeled vehicles was unknown in the Americas. In this claim they are on reasonably safe ground. What they neglect to take into consideration is that there were no draught animals available in the Americas to draw such wheeled vehicles. The use of such vehicles in Europe was hastened by the presence of such draught animals as oxen, donkeys, and horses. All three were absent in the Americas.

It has been pointed out that the sledge not only is a much more ancient method of moving materials from one place to another, but, in places where neither wheeled vehicles nor draught animals are available, is the common and accepted manner of transporting bulky materials either over snow or dry ground. Even when draught animals have been available, variations of the sledge have been used in place of wheeled vehicles. Well into the present century there were many farming areas in North America where a wheel-less vehicle, a kind of sledge commonly called a "stone-boat," was used for removing boulders from farm fields, in both winter and summer. It is reasonable to assume that the Maya and other civilized peoples of the Americas employed a similar method.

Erich von Däniken, author of a sensational best-seller *Chariots of the Gods?* sums up, perhaps unintentionally, the uncritical and uninformed European viewpoint of the handicaps under which a wheel-less civilization laboured:

> Anyone who arrived among the Mayas from the ancient world would have known about the wheel for transporting men and objects. Surely one of the first actions of a sage, a god like Quetzalcoatl, who appeared as missionary, lawgiver, doctor, and adviser on many practical aspects of life, would have been to instruct the poor Mayas in the use of the wheel and the cart. In fact the Mayas never used either.

Herr von Däniken's crocodile tears may move many to sympathy for the lot of the hapless Maya. They will leave unmoved any who have seen and joyed in the magnificent facade of the Palace of the Governor at Uxmal. The lack of wheels and draught animals posed no obstacles for the civilized people of Middle America who raised, with sledges and log rollers and ropes, some of the most tremendous edifices on earth.

Again and again I have read the statement that the wheel was unknown in ancient America. Such a belief was for many years an article of faith among archaeologists. Anyone who challenged it was subjected to the withering scorn of the academic community. The first to encounter the searing blast of professional disdain was the extraordinary French explorer and archaeological dilettante, Désiré Charnay.

Charnay was fascinated by the Toltecs. Like Heinrich Schliemann, who believed that the Homeric legends concealed true history and by following his heart found ancient Troy, Charnay listened to the legend of Prince Topiltzin, believed it, and found the long-lost Tula. Schliemann was a rich man, able to indulge his whims. When he found Troy he was able to force the learned world to accept his discovery. Charnay was only an employee of the French Ministry of Public Instruction. When he announced that he had found Tula, there was a deafening silence from academe. It was not until 1940 – long after Charnay's death – that excavations begun at his site proved that he had indeed discovered the great legendary city of the Toltecs.

Charnay had even worse luck with wheels. In the 1880's he was carrying out a rather amateurish dig 13,000 feet up in the Monte del Fraile within view of the great pyramid at Cholula, one of the "cities of Quetzalcoatl." There he found a cemetery which he believed to belong to his favourite ancient people, the Toltecs. Digging into some of the many graves, he found a number of strange little toys made of terracotta. Some of them represented animals, elongated dogs and coyotes. They had wheels. The axles were missing. Being of wood, they had rotted away. There were also little carts – Charnay called them "chariots" – their wheels lying uselessly beside them. Charnay whittled little axles of wood and inserted them into the holes in the wheels and in the terracotta stumps hollowed out to receive them. "Behold!" wrote Charnay. "My chariots rolled!"

The world of professional archaeology said Charnay's toys were obviously modern fabrications. Charnay said his good name had been insulted, but the wind swallowed his words and he died unvindicated.

In 1940 an expedition under Matthew W. Stirling began excavating at Tres Zapotes in the State of Vera Cruz – Olmec country. There they found eight little clay wheels lying alongside a little pottery dog and a pottery jaguar. The archaeologists repeated Charnay's experiment. Wooden sticks were inserted into clay tubes on the bodies of the animals and the wheels were attached. Behold, the toys rolled!

Since 1940 a number of similar artifacts have been found in the Mexican states of Vera Cruz and Oaxaca and in the Isthmus of Panama.

So the ancient peoples of Middle America not only knew the principle of the wheel but had adapted it to use – for toys.

Two questions immediately present themselves – from whom did they learn the principle, and why was it not employed in a more practical manner? Neither question can be answered with absolutes. I can say that Quetzalcoatl, the stranger from the east, taught them, but I cannot prove it. I submit, however, that there are powerful hints that an overseas alien was responsible for these startling discoveries. Charnay's find was made at Cholula, where the cult of the Feathered Serpent was very strong. The Tres Zapotes and other Gulf Coast finds of wheeled toys occurred in an area where portrait heads of non-Indian types have also been found. It will be remembered that the Tres Zapotes site also yielded the Mephistophelian clay head of which Matthew Stirling said: "It is probably a study of a prominent person." This is also the area where persistent tradition states that the culture-hero made his land-fall. Can pure coincidence stretch so far? Yet coincidence has been offered as explanation for all these striking phenomena. As Lord Byron said in *Don Juan:*

A "strange coincidence" to use a phrase
By which such things are settled now-a-days.

The second question has already been answered in part. The principle of the wheel was not employed in carts or other wheeled vehicles because there were in Middle America no draught animals to pull them. It is true that men could have pulled wheeled vehicles more easily than sledges, but such a change might have affected the basic structure of Middle American technology and hence would have proved unacceptable to the minds of the American natives of the second century A.D.

This last statement requires clarification. It is admittedly difficult for the twentieth-century representative of Western civilization to accept the fact that peoples less technologically advanced than himself are unable immediately to recognize the superior merits of his ways. Yet scientific observations carried out in many areas of the world in this century have shown that less advanced cultures will nearly always reject any innovations that call for a basic restructuring of their society. Kaj Birket-Smith, the Danish ethnologist, in his book *The Paths of Culture* (University of Wisconsin Press: 1965[1]) uses the example of the contacts between the modern culture of New Guinea and the natives of Australia:

The Australian aborigines have in later periods borrowed compara-tively insignificant things such as bark belts and conch horns from New Guinea, but have adopted improved fishing methods only to a very limited degree. This seemingly paradoxical situation can probably be explained by the fact that precisely because they are rather trivial the bark belts and conch horns can be fitted into the general cultural pattern, whereas fishing is so deeply rooted in the culture, both socially and religiously, that new methods would call for a recasting of the entire structure.

This experience, repeated again and again in many parts of the world where Iron Age and Stone Age societies have collided, explains precisely why the principle of the wheel as applied to wheeled vehicles resulted, on its introduction into Middle America, in nothing more than children's toys. It is quite possible that the first such toy was made by the culture-hero or one of his comrades as a demonstration of the practical application of the wheel. If so, it failed in its purpose. The application of such a revolutionary development would have called for an almost total revamping of the native technology, already closely identified with the social and religious structures of their society. And so the wheel, introduced from its birthplace, the Eurasian continent, remained in Middle America a piece of civilized bric-a-brac, a novelty, a toy for children.

The argument here advanced to account for the non-introduction of the wheeled vehicle into ancient America can also, of course, be applied to the matter of the key-stone arch. Even if any of the accidental voyagers had been able to apply the principle in practice, it would have been resisted by the native population precisely because it would have entailed a basic change in their way of doing things.

It must be pointed out, however, that the great city of Teotihuacán – allegedly a foundation of Quetzalcoatl – represents in itself a basic and significant break with native tradition. It has been noted that most of the so-called "cities" of the New World were actually only ceremonial centres serving largely rural populations. Teotihuacán was apparently thoroughly urbanized – a city in the European sense, in which not only the priests and administrators lived, but also the artisans and the common people. This change was effected, it is said, under the rule of the culture-hero. The date for the change, as given by the archaeological specialists, was the first half of the second century A.D.

How did this come about? How was native conservatism overcome in this instance? I think it was all quite simply done and not by the imposition of any alien plan, previously announced and determined upon.

Teotihuacán was a religious foundation. Much evidence exists to show that the temples were built by the rural populations probably on a voluntary basis during that part of the year when their labour was not required on the land. Teotihuacán was the most ambitious project ever undertaken by a Mexican population up to that time. The building of the great central complex must have taken the work of a generation. Colonies of artisans would have sprung up on the site. In time, having developed special functions, they may have stayed on to maintain the site and so have become true urbanites. Much the same process took place, a few centuries later, in connection with the building of the great Gothic cathedrals of Europe. The motivating force in both cases was the same – to build great soaring structures to the greater glory of God.

Chapter Eleven

COINS AND INSCRIPTIONS

> All passes. Art alone
>   Enduring stays to us;
> The Bust outlasts the throne,—
>   The coin, Tiberius.

> — Henry Austin Dobson (1840-1921)

From time to time since the first permanent European settlements were made in the Americas, discoveries have been made which reinforce the theory of an early contact between the peoples of the two shores of the Atlantic Ocean. Most of these finds have been made in a random fashion. Some are of dubious authenticity. Some have been attributed, by zealous *aficionados* of the unusual, to the ancient Phoenicians (dates generally unspecified); the Irish under St. Brendan (486-578 A.D.); many to the Norsemen (1000-1350 A.D.); some to Prince Madoc of Wales (twelfth century A.D.) and a few to Earl Sinclair, Prince of the Orkneys (fourteenth century).

In the great majority of cases, these discoveries have consisted of single artifacts, architectural complexes, or apparent linguistic parallels. Among the artifactual examples that may be cited are the carved rock in the Taunton river near Dighton, Massachusetts, the characters of which were first interpreted as Phoenician and later, by the unscrupulous addition of a few lines, as a Norse inscription; the ruined structures found in New Hampshire and Massachusetts, credited by some enthusiasts to Irish monks of the Culdee order; the squat tower at Newport, Rhode Island, attributed to the Vikings; and a carving on a rock at Westford, Massachusetts, said to depict a mediaeval knight bearing on his shield armorial insignia identified as the blazonry of the

Orkney Sinclairs, lieges of the Norwegian throne in the fourteenth century.

In the present state of our knowledge of the history of the Americas in the pre-Columbian period it would be folly to dismiss out of hand all or any of these claims. However, the embarrassing revelations of the hoaxes of the Piltdown Skull in England and the Kensington, Minnesota, rune stone in the United States have made all scholars doubly cautious. A single artifact or a single site are poor materials on which to erect a theory when the possibilities of deliberate or unintentional fakery are so high.

In biblical scholarship there are two kinds of interpretation of sacred scripture: one is called exegesis, the second, hermeneutics. Exegesis is concerned with the practical exposition of a given text in terms of the lives or understanding of those subjected to the interpretation; hermeneutics is the art or science of the interpretation of the text itself. The first is subjective, the second, objective. If the Newport Tower, the North Salem "beehives," and the Dighton rock are looked upon as texts in stone, then it must be confessed that much of the interpretation of these curiosities has been exegetical in nature rather than hermeneutical; subjective rather than objective.

Among the random harvests of the soil of the Americas only one group, in my opinion, merits consideration as objective evidence. The number of objects involved, the fact that most were found under reasonably certifiable conditions, and their probable geographical and chronological origins fit in very well with a postulated transatlantic traffic within the first four centuries of the Christian era.

The evidence presented in this chapter comes from five widely separated areas of the New World – Brazil, Venezuela, the Mexican states of Yucatan and Baja California, and the states of Kentucky and Tennessee in the United States. Of the datable artifacts, the chronological range is from the beginning of the Christian era to 350 A.D. The general provenance of all is the Mediterranean basin, with special emphasis on the eastern end of that sea. The evidence offered consists of two kinds: objects made, inscribed, or painted in the Americas, and artifacts demonstrably made elsewhere, specifically on the European continent. The latter are scientifically the more significant, since they can be dated.

One of the early finds was that made by John Haywood, Chief Justice of the Supreme Court of Tennessee. The discovery was reported in *Niles' Weekly Register* (Philadelphia) in its issue of August 22, 1818. The find consisted of three Roman coins, one of which a numismatist identified from the description as being a denarius of the reign of the Emperor Antoninus Pius (138-161 A.D.). Later in his book *Natural and Aboriginal History of Tennessee* (Nashville: 1823), Justice Haywood identified a second coin as having been minted in the reign of the Emperor Commodus (180-192 A.D.). Unfortunately, these coins are not now available for examination.

Much more recently coins have been dug up in the neighbouring state of Kentucky at Louisville (1932), Clay City (1952), and Hopkinsville (1967). These coins, which remain available for examination, all bear Hebrew inscriptions which identify them as having been minted during the last Jewish rebellion against Rome (132-135 A.D.) under the leadership of Simon Bar Kokhba.

A hoard of several hundred Roman coins dating from the reign of Augustus (27 B.C. –14 A.D.) to that of Constans I (337-350 A.D.) has been reported found in a pottery vessel buried in the sand on the coast of Venezuela. It has been speculated that the coins, now at the Smithsonian Institution in Washington, D.C., represented the ready cash of a Roman trader shipwrecked on the Caribbean coast.

One such numismatic discovery might be discounted; five cannot be shrugged off. There undoubtedly have been other such finds, for which I have no specific details.

The evidence offered by the coins is buttressed by a group of inscriptions, also found in widely separated areas, which have been painted, pecked, or carved in characters which have been identified as European in origin. Two of the most important discoveries made in this field have been exhaustively examined by Dr. Cyrus H. Gordon, chairman of the Department of Mediterranean Studies at Brandeis University.[1] Scientifically more important is Dr. Gordon's analysis of an engraved stone found in a burial mound at Bat Creek, Loudon County, in eastern Tennessee by an expedition from the Smithsonian Institution in the 1880's. The discovery was first reported by Cyrus Thomas in the *Twelfth Annual Report of the Bureau of Ethnology to the Secretary of the Smithsonian Institution 1890-91*. The pertinent passage reads as follows:

Nothing of interest was discovered until the bottom was reached, where nine skeletons were found lying on the original surface of the ground, surrounded by dark colored earth. These were disposed as shown in Fig. 272. No. 1 lying at full length with the head south, and close by, parallel with it, but with the head north, was No. 2. On the same level were seven others, all close side by side, with heads north and in a line. All were badly decayed. No relics were found with any but No. 1, immediately under the skull and jaw bones of which were two copper bracelets, an engraved stone, a small drilled fossil, a copper bead, a bone implement, and some small pieces of polished wood . . . . The engraved stone lay partially under the back part of the skull and was struck by the steel rod used in probing.

The report was illustrated by two figures showing the disposition of the skeletons and a facsimile of the inscribed stone which Thomas identified as being in the Cherokee script (first devised in 1821). The identification went unchallenged for nearly seventy years until a scholar, the late Dr. W. W. Strong, observed that if the published inscription were turned the other side up, the script was identifiably "Phoenician." Some years later, Dr. Henriette Mertz in her book *The Wine Dark Sea* (Chicago: 1964) came to the same conclusion and identified two of the letters. Dr. Joseph B. Mahan in 1970 identified a sequence of five letters as "Canaanite." It remained for Dr. Gordon to recognize the script as Hebrew and to establish a tentative translation as "Year One of the Comet for Judea," that is, the dawn of the Golden Age. The meaning of the two vertical lines followed by a dot at the top of the inscription remains enigmatic. It has been suggested that each stroke stands for the Hebrew letter "nun" which means fish and that the double use indicates the zodiacal sign, Pisces, usually represented as two fish. I should like to point out that the sign of two fish also has a Christian significance, one frequently employed in the early days of the Christian community.[2]

Dr. Gordon has also certified as authentic an inscribed stone found near Paraiba, Brazil, in 1872. The inscription, at first thought to be Phoenician and later described as a forgery, has been interpreted by Dr. Gordon as recounting the adventures of the crew and passengers (fifteen in all, twelve men and three women) of a vessel which became separated from its nine companion ships during a circumnavigation of Africa in 531 B.C. During a storm at sea, the ship was captured by the South Equatorial Current and carried to the shores of Brazil.

101

More recently a strange find was made in the ruins of a sixteenth-century Spanish church in the village of Tihosuco, Yucatan. Robert Marx reported on the find in the April 1973 issue of *Argosy* :

> In the spring of 1971, while on an expedition with Milt Machlin, the editor of ARGOSY . . . we noticed that a large stone lintel over a doorway in the church had an inscription carved into it. Expecting the inscription to be in Spanish or Latin, I was amazed to find upon closer inspection that it was in some strange writing which was not Mayan hieroglyphics; I knew we were onto something important. Dr. Cyrus Gordon has identified the script from photographs as belonging to some ancient form of Mediterranean writing – possibly Phoenician. Apparently the stone was found by a Spaniard or Indian and incorporated into the building of the church.

Some 1,800 airline miles to the northwest of Tihosuco, near the Mission of San Fernando Velicata, Baja California, there is a short inscription embodying characters some of which strikingly resemble those in the Tihosuco find. The arrangement of eight signs in a line at the top of the petroglyph make it quite clear that we are dealing with a form of writing, not just a collection of random geometrical figures. The style of the characters most nearly resembles that of the Cypriote syllabary, a linear script of some forty-five symbols developed at an early time on the Island of Cyprus, perhaps from a still earlier Minoan prototype. Of the symbols used David Diringer[3] says:

> These are made up of combinations of strokes, straight, semi-circular and circular which gives the entire syllabary a somewhat geometric appearance.

Beneath the leading inscription of San Fernando is a group of a score of very strange symbols, one of which resembles a sign used at Tihosuco. This entire section of the petroglyph is separated from the remaining portion by two irregularly parallel lines running from the top right to the lower left. To the right of the second line is another group of characters which has been described as "a reasonable facsimile of a Roman numeral." If this was the intended interpretation, the figure could be 24 (XXIV). Whether this is so or not, the whole petroglyph conveys a distinct impression of having been intended as a map, with the uninscribed space between the vertical lines graphically indicating a body of water – a stream, a river, a bay, or an ocean.

The San Fernando site is not the only one in Baja California containing specimens of rock art indicating that at one time this barren peninsula supported, or at least hosted, a population with an advanced culture. The Spanish friars were particularly impressed with this evidence since the natives they found there on their arrival in the early eighteenth century were at the very bottom rung of human society – naked, possessing only the most rudimentary form of societal structure, eking out a bare subsistence in a parched, rocky desert.

Don Francisco Javier Clavigero, S.J., reported in 1790 having found a cave painting near the Mission of San Joaquin (inland from Santa Rosalia, on the coast of the Gulf of California) which represented "men and women with garments similar to those of the Mexicans, but they were entirely barefoot. The men had their arms open and somewhat elevated." I find the last sentence of this description especially intriguing since the attitude of the arms of the figures adequately describes the ancient Hebrew form of approaching God in prayer.

While none of the Baja California examples of cave art have been given a date, there are some obvious differences in style which probably indicate intervals of time. At one site, for instance, an illustration of a group of people approaching two pine trees is within the recognizable tradition of Indian rock art. Again, the use of the well-known Moki (Hopi) rain sign – a cloud from which drops are falling – indicates the presence of at least some American natives among the persons responsible for the petroglyphs.

However, the petroglyphs in the Arroyo Grande, forty miles northwest of San Felipe as well as those at San Fernando, contain characters that are distinctively non-Indian. In the Arroyo Grande there are found, in addition to the Moki rain sign, characters that may be identified as the Greek letters "*chi*" and "*rho.*" Since the days of the early Christian Church, these letters have been used as the monogram of Christ, from the first two letters of XPICTOC (Christos).

Also readily identifiable in the inscription are a letter M which may be either Greek or Latin and two symbols which may be found in the Cypriote syllabary.

In approaching the identification of characters and the tentative translation of enigmatic inscriptions such as those in the Arroyo Grande and at the San Fernando mission, one should not expect to find literary historical documents. The strangers who laboriously carved or pecked out these records were not interested in recording for posterity their own names or the year in which they arrived in that desolate place, but rather *what* they were and in whose Name they came there. I have a distinct feeling that this is what the artists of the Arroyo Grande were trying to tell us.

The foregoing four paragraphs have been exegetical in nature. Let us return to hermeneutics.

The chronological range of the datable artifacts mentioned in this brief summary is from 531 B.C. (accepting Dr. Gordon's reading of the Paraiba inscription) to 350 A.D. (the approximate date of the latest coin in the Venezuela hoard). Both end dates imply accidental voyages terminated by shipwrecks. The middle range – represented by the Kentucky and Tennessee coins – is from 135 to 192 A.D. These finds were made far inland and infer not only a voyage on the ocean but a long journey by land.

As Dr. Cottie Burland, Geoffrey Ashe, J.V. Luce, Thor Heyerdahl, and others have pointed out, accidental drift voyages across the Atlantic have been possible at any time since the eighteenth century B.C. when Crete became the first great maritime civilization. That such voyages did, in fact, take place can hardly be disputed. The number of survivors of such voyages would have been small since their vessels would not have been provisioned for such a lengthy journey. The influence of the survivors on the native populations would have been minimal and geographically limited, especially if the landfall were made among peoples at a low level of cultural development as would have been the case in the coastal regions of Brazil and Venezuela in the last six centuries B.C. and the first four centuries A.D.

On the other hand, the archaeological evidence from Mexico, extending from Baja California on the west to Yucatan on the east and in the inland states of Kentucky and Tennessee in the United States strongly indicates the presence not of a handful of survivors, but of a considerable number of Mediterraneans, notably Semitic in racial character, wielding a widespread influence, particularly in the field of religious beliefs and observances.

The "Phoenician" landing in Brazil and the "Roman" landfall in Venezuela may be dismissed as historical oddities. The evidence from Yucatan, Calixtlahuaca, Baja California, Kentucky, and Tennessee cannot be dealt with so cavalierly. Here we are dealing with materials dating back in general to the second century A.D., scattered over an extensive area by people with an Eastern Mediterranean background

104

carrying both Jewish and Roman currency, observing the Hebrew attitude of prayer and with a knowledge of Roman, Greek, and Semitic alphabetic and syllabic characters.

The range of dates represented by these artifacts and their wide geographical distribution cannot be the result of a single "drift" voyage. Rather, they strongly indicate the existence in the second Christian century of a transatlantic traffic by sizable numbers of deliberate adventurers, refugees, and intending colonists, driven by crises to dare the Atlantic with the hope of finding a new home elsewhere.

If the evidence of the Bar Kokhba and the Roman coins is accepted, we must postulate at least *two* east-west crossings of the Atlantic in that significant century – one ending on the shores of the Gulf of Mexico, the other far in the interior of the United States of America. As we shall see, there were, in fact, two crises among the Jewish people in the second century sufficiently desperate to send men into the unknown in a final gamble for peace and security.

PART III

THE CULTURAL
EVIDENCE

Chapter Twelve

THE MONOTHEISTIC TRADITION

Admirable is the account of the time in which it came to pass that all was formed in heaven and upon earth, the quartering of their signs, their measurement and alignment, and the establishment of parallels to the skies and upon the earth to the four quarters thereof, as was spoken by the Creator and Maker, the Mother, the Father of life and of all existence, that one by whom all move and breathe, father and sustainer of the peace of peoples, by whose wisdom was premeditated the excellence of all that doth exist in the heavens, upon the earth, in lake and sea.

— The *Popol Vuh* of the Quiché-Maya.

In our efforts to unravel the mystery of the great culture-hero of the Americas, we have so far considered three different kinds of evidence.

Our starting point was the legend itself. Its persistence through more than a thousand years of the pre-Columbian history of the American continents and the recurrence over an enormous geographical area of certain basic and significant details of the epic certainly entitle it to serious investigation as the reflection of a possible historical event. Legend by itself is subject to many interpretations and, considered as history, is inevitably suspect. However, we have seen that independent evidence of a factual nature has reinforced the evidence of the legend. Legend says that the culture-hero introduced a new religious faith. Archaeological discoveries have indicated quite strongly that there was in fact a widespread revolution in religious thought occurring in those very areas where the epic of the hero-god was strongest and that this event happened sometime in the first five Christian centuries, most probably originating in the first or second centuries.[1]

Archaeological evidence again has presented us with a number of artifacts hinting strongly at the presence among the largely smooth-faced and beardless natives of a group of bearded men of non-Indian appearance. While not all of these artifacts have been positively dated, many fall roughly within the first five Christian centuries.

Finally, in an area where these bearded images most powerfully provoke the assumption that they are portraits of living persons known to the artists, two objects had been found which have been identified by some European specialists as being of Roman manufacture, dating to the second century A.D. Additionally, Roman and Jewish coins and a Hebrew inscription date to the same period.

The evidence I have presented to this point has been discussed, debated, and argued over with varying degrees of heat for some years. Tentative conclusions have been advanced, none of which has been satisfactory or widely accepted. This has been so in my view because a very important element in the mystery has not been sufficiently investigated.

I have, I think, made it clear that I consider the Quetzalcoatl legend and its attendant archaeological evidence as pointing towards the possibility of a transatlantic, European, Judaeo-Christian contact with the Americas early in the Christian era. If we are seriously to consider this possibility then obviously the religious element in the evidence must be carefully examined. One of the problems in this field has been that the surviving evidence of pre-Columbian religious thought has been evaluated almost exclusively by specialists in disciplines unrelated to the history of religion. With all due respect I submit that a specialist in pottery sequences is no more qualified to judge the spiritual values of the people who used the pottery than is a professional minister of religion to rule on the firing techniques employed in making the pottery.

The pottery specialist, the practical archaeologist on the dig, the soil specialist, the sociologist, the anthropologist, the ethnologist, the folk-lorist, and all the other specialists perform invaluable functions in the collection and evaluation of the evidence within their specific disci-plines. Without their evidence we would be very much in the dark as to how thought processes worked in societies which have left few or no written records. There is, however, a lamentable lack of cross-fertil-ization between and among these disciplines. Each specialist can only provide a partial picture of the past, based upon his specialty and limited by his personal bias. There is as yet little being done in the way of providing overall interpretations of the totality of information and impressions gained by the specialists in their study of a given society or individual site.

Nowhere is this lack more evident than when a specialist in one of the acknowledged disciplines attempts to evaluate his findings in terms of the optimum spiritual aspirations of the people studied. I say "optimum spiritual aspirations," for there has always been a pronounced difference between the statements and beliefs of the leaders of religious thought in any given society and the religious practices of the mass of the people in that society. The French theologian, Charles Guignebert, summarized most succinctly this schism between the religion of the élite and the practices of the common folk in his *Ancient, Medieval and Modern Christianity* :[2]

> Instinctively, or, if you like it better thus, from a mental incapacity to act otherwise, the populace that has not learned, and does not know how to reflect always cleaves . . . to religious conceptions and practices which do not correspond exactly either with the teachings of the recognized religion, nor with the mentality of its learned ministrants, nor yet with the conception of its dogmas and tenets which prevails among enlightened believers. This popular religion, when analyzed, is revealed as a syncretism, a medley of beliefs and customs, differing in origin, age and meaning, and only existing side by side because those who accept them never compare them . . . . The people, especially the rural populations, never make a clean sweep of their religious beliefs and rites; they spontaneously adapt them to the new religion imposed upon them, or else, should this religion refuse to entertain them, they drive them further back into the recesses of their consciousness and the depths of their inner being, where they remain as active superstitions.

This comment by the great French scholar is particularly important when we come to study the history of religion in the Americas prior to the arrival of the Spanish Christian missionaries. The folklore of the native peoples which has been assiduously gathered for more than four centuries represents quite clearly the religious thoughts, practices, and ethics of the masses of the societies studied. They by no means necessarily represent the optimum spiritual aspirations of their religious leaders and teachers, any more than do the popular astrology columns in our newspapers represent the highest spiritual attainments of twentieth-century man. When, therefore, we are confronted by some of the truly horrendous gods of the Aztec pantheon, we are not thereby justified in concluding that the bloody sacrifices they demanded are the highest expressions of Aztec spiritual thought. For this we must turn to some of the pitiably few fragments of prayer and poetry left by the great priests and teachers of that people:

> Dost thou think, perhaps, my heart, thou shalt live on the earth alone?
> Thou art anguished, heart of mine. I was born upon earth.
> Art thou thine own friend, perhaps?
> Dost thou live perhaps for thyself?
> Be thou, god, on my side; mould me!
> Recreate thy breast, appease thy heart, make thy heart glad! [3]

This dichotomy between religious thought and religious practice should present no insuperable mental obstacles to the members of a twentieth-century society which is nominally, if remotely, Christian.

And so the few surviving scraps of religious literature give us a picture of the beliefs of the spiritual élite which is greatly at variance with what we know of the popular religion as expressed in the folk mythology of pre-Columbian America. The mythologies of the American tribes have been raked over again and again and again. We know virtually every little superstition and superstitious practice of the aboriginal population of these continents. We know how the priests of the native tribes satisfied the common people's need of amulets and magic signs to ward off the evil eye and the destruction often wrought by natural forces. However, no one, so far as I know, has yet attempted to deal with the purely religious aspects of the cult of Quetzalcoatl, which represents most surely the optimum spiritual aspirations of the peoples of Mexico and Middle and South America.

There are enormous problems to be encountered in such an investigation. There was a gap of 1,400 years between the introduction of the Quetzalcoatl cult and the contact with it by modern Christian influences. Whatever theological concepts were introduced in the second century were bound to have been adulterated and altered in the course of a millenium and a half even if the native societies had been stable throughout those centuries, which they were not.

In addition, the priesthood would have found it necessary from time to time (as priesthoods always have) to adapt their personal beliefs to the limited understanding of their people. Rushton Coulborn in *The Origin of Civilized Societies* (Princeton: 1959) explains in this way the slow changes in the popular understanding of the Quetzalcoatl cult.

The association of the rain-gods with the corn-god were only two among an enormous number of associations which show clearly how important the pervasive rain-gods were. *Many of these associations were probably comparatively late developments effected by the priests as they enlarged the theology in order to hold the popular imagination* ... Quetzalcoatl's original character may have been his character as culture-hero, but he became identified with the east wind which brought to Mexico its beneficent rain supply from the Gulf and consequently his relation with the Tlaloque became a close one. (Italics mine.)

The association between Quetzalcoatl and the east wind led to the erection of such round pyramids and temples as the Caracol at Chichén Itzá in Yucatan and the temple of Quetzalcoatl at Calixtlahuaca. These were dedicated to the hero in his aspect as Ehecatl in which his beard degenerates into something resembling a duck's bill.[4]

As I have mentioned before, the attention of the Spanish friars in the sixteenth century was first focused not so much on the theology of the native priesthood as on certain liturgical practices which seemed strongly reminiscent of Christian rites. There was observed, in some areas of the New World, a communal meal resembling in many respects the Holy Eucharist. Fasting was a common usage among the Aztecs. There was widespread observance of the rites of baptism with water, confession, absolution, and penance. Some of the surviving invitations to confession and prayers of absolution are strikingly similar to Christian use.

Two criticisms may with justice be made of this evidence. In the first place it is difficult to be absolutely certain in all instances that the materials cited are free of possible sixteenth-century Christian influence. There may have been, and undoubtedly were, cases where the native tradition was altered to please, or appease, the Spanish friars. To this criticism one can only reply that there do remain, after the most searching scrutiny, enough undeniably pre-Columbian records to testify to the existence of most of the liturgical practices mentioned above, as well as some of the prayers, at a date well before the advent of the *conquistadores*. The second criticism applies directly to the rites said to have been observed by the native populations. Rituals involving purification by water are common in many societies throughout the world and are by no means exclusively Christian. Practices of confession, absolution, and penance have appeared also among non-Christian societies. Indeed, many of the concepts respecting water purification, rebirth of the soul, and so on are common, for obvious reasons, to agricultural societies everywhere.

The idea of the communal meal may go back to very primitive times. It may be that the cannibalistic meals of Peking man 400,000 years ago were not occasioned by the lack of other food but by a desire to achieve the qualities and strength of the deceased. Certainly this seems to have been the meaning of the appalling cannibalism practised by the Aztecs on selected sacrificial victims.

It can be argued that all the liturgical practices observed in Middle America can be traced to a common, universal pool of spirituality. Joseph Campbell in his magnificent study of world mythology, *The Masks of God*, has exposed the psychic unity of much of mankind's spiritual symbology.[5]

However valid these criticisms may be, they do not, and cannot, account for the appearance of a whole constellation of liturgical practices resembling Christian rites in a setting and at a time coincident with the archaeological evidence of a religious revolution and with the legendary arrival of the leader of that revolution.

Here and there, in the accumulated evidence, are found striking clues to the nature of that revolutionary movement. In Yucatan, for instance, it was reported by Diego de Landa that the rites of baptism, confession, and absolution were administered only once at the point of death. This was a common practice of the primitive Christian church until its abuse led to strictures against it. Charles Guignebert explained the reasoning behind the practice:

> Such emphasis is laid on the rigour of the engagements entered into in baptism and of the peril involved in their violation, that many men who are perfectly good Christians at heart consider it both more comfortable and more prudent to ask for baptism only when at the point of death.[6]

There were obvious dangers in such postponements. Cases are recorded where the candidate for baptism died before the arrival of the priest. Terrified at the prospect of eternal damnation for the deceased, a member of the family or a friend would hide under the bed and give the required responses for the dead man, while the priest baptized a corpse.

Such abuses as these, Guignebert says, reached a peak in the third and fourth centuries and led to strong measures by the church to check them.

Such anomalies as this, seen in the framework of sixteenth-century Spanish Roman Catholicism, led Diego de Landa and other church authorities to condemn the seeming Christian rites as pagan deviltries. In the light of our own present knowledge of the history of the primitive Christian church, they serve an opposite purpose, strengthening the impression of a Christian foundation in Mexico early in the Christian era.

Some linguistic evidence also points to theological concepts resembling Christianity. The Mayan language in de Landa's day contained separate words for soul, *ol*, and purged soul, *ce-ol*. I find it significant that so many of the practices and beliefs of the cult of Quetzalcoatl focused on acts of purification – baptism with water, confession, and absolution – features strongly emphasized as well in the early Christian church.

Yet, when all of this evidence has been weighed up, we are left with some nagging doubts about the absolute authenticity of the data the friars collected from the natives while the old practices were still being followed.

There are no such doubts when it comes to what I consider to be the most extraordinary development of all – the sudden emergence in many places in the Western Hemisphere of a monotheistic religious philosophy beginning about the second century A.D. This is supported by the full weight of archaeological research. This was a vast leap forward in religious thought. It has been accomplished rarely in history and always with very great difficulty. In witness one may offer the abortive attempt at monotheism by the Pharaoh Amenhotep IV, more generally known by the cognomen Akhnaton, which he adopted in honour of his "one, single god," the beneficent disc of the sun. The Hebrew leader Moses and his successors introduced the concept but only, as the Torah testifies, against the powerful opposition of a people long attached to their tribal gods, their Elohim. It was not until the times of the brilliant Second Isaiah (the Book of Isaiah, Chapters 40 to 55) in the sixth century B.C. that the idea of a *universal* creator god seized the imagination of the Jewish people.

Yet in the Americas of the second century A.D. we find this advanced concept being adopted by whole native populations – or at least by their priesthood – in one of the most extraordinary, innovative religious developments the world has ever seen. Nothing that we know of in the previous histories of the people prepares us for this event. All the evidence points to a simple, primitive form of worship of the forces of nature, involving in most cases animal totems.

The evidence seems unassailable that the bearers of this new faith were aliens to the affected communities. What they introduced was remarkably enduring. Obviously, over the course of centuries there were revivals of the old, popular beliefs. I believe that further research will one day establish that there were instances of the new priesthood being overthrown from time to time by popular, secular revolutions against local theocracies. Nevertheless, although many compromises with the popular beliefs were undoubtedly made, the worship of one supreme god remained a persistent feature of New World religion right up to the Conquest.

Walter Krickeberg[7] points out that "the great god of Mexico shares many of the attributes possessed by the supreme being in other religions." The Aztecs regarded him as the only "true god," *nelli teotl*, omnipresent, and intangible as "night and wind." The worship of the one true god required no temples. He demanded of his worshippers "only piety, humility and exemplary conduct; he was worshipped only in prayer."

This approach to the All-Father is found not only in Mexico but throughout the Americas. There are nowhere to be found temples directly connected with his worship; yet that worship is a golden thread running through the tapestry of American native religions as a constant motif. Even in tribes far removed geographically from the scenes of the first revelation the principle of the supreme god is found in good health after the European invasion of the Americas, as in the case of the Great Manitou of the Iroquoian peoples in North America.

In sum then, we are left with the unquestioned evidence of a strong monotheistic influence dating to the beginning of the Christian era, imported into the affected communities at complete variance with previous religious practices; a group of liturgical rites which bear marked resemblance to early Christian practices and linguistic traces of theological terms of unusual sophistication.

A word must now be said about symbols. Some early observers attached significance to the abundance of crosses used in the temples. The crosses in many instances pre-date the Christian period and are of no value as evidence of Christian contact. Crosses of different designs are found everywhere in the world among primitive peoples. It is undoubtedly one of the earliest symbols used by mankind and has many meanings. Among the Maya and, later, the Aztecs, it was often used as a representation of the tree of life – another very ancient concept. An amazingly sophisticated Mayan interpretation interprets the cross as the "intersection of time and space." I do not know if this interpretation is provably pre-Columbian; it marches well with the very advanced Mayan mathematical ideas.

In connection with the theory advanced in this book, the presence or absence of the cross symbol has no significance. If the contact which I have postulated occurred at the time I have suggested, the cross would not have been in extensive use as a symbol of the new faith. Not until the third and fourth centuries did the symbol of Christ's sacrifice receive universal application as the sign of Christian membership. In the second century the more common symbols of the new faith were fish, bread, sheaves of wheat, shells, water symbols, and sheep.

I find significant the common use of water and fish symbols in connection with the cult of Quetzalcoatl. Maize obviously replaced the wheat and bread symbols of the Old World. The so-called "young maize god" was frequently represented with a cross or "tree of life" growing out of his body. It is a symbol of rebirth, of re-creation, or resurrection.

So important did Hermann Leicht find the widespread use of the fish symbol in South America that he felt the discovery of the reasons for its use would open a whole new volume of the history of the ancient peoples of that continent.

Altogether, what has been discovered and reported about the cult of Quetzalcoatl is compatible with its having been a Christian foundation. But if the foundation is Christian, where is the Christ? He is present certainly in the ritual practices usually associated with the church that bears his name, but nowhere in the legends is there any specific reference to an identifiable Christ figure. If there originally was such a figure in the teachings of Quetzalcoatl, his attributes came to be associated with the person of his missionary, the hero-god himself. Quetzalcoatl was the person whom the first generation of converts had known and revered. It was he of whom they could have said, "which we have seen with our eyes, which we have looked upon and our hands have handled." [8] With the passing of the centuries and their attendant strife and civil disorder, only the missionary was remembered and his message of love and brotherhood. The culture-hero was worshipped as a god in later years precisely for those attributes which are normally associated in Western society with the figure of Jesus of Nazareth, the Christ.

Now, if I am correct in assuming that the members of this second-century, transatlantic missionary venture taught the faith which came to be called Christian, an unanswered question remains: What Christ did they teach? This is a very important question. The second century, particularly the first half of that century, was the formative period in the history of the Christian church. The New Testament canon was not fixed, nor would it be for another two centuries. The Gospel According to St. Mark and possibly that of St. Matthew as well were in circulation, but not necessarily in the form in which they have come down to us. Modern scholarship has revealed many emendations and additions by later hands in these works. There is no agreement on the dates for the writing of The Gospel According to St. Luke and its sequel, The Book of the Acts of the Apostles. The guesses range from 80 A.D. to 150 A.D. The Gospel According to St. John was almost certainly not composed until the dawn of the second century.

In the period with which we are concerned, the letters of St. Paul were circulating among the Gentile churches of Europe and Asia Minor. It is important to realize that these letters represent a different and conflicting tradition. They reflect the thinking of their author who was the true founder of what is today called the "Christian" church. This brilliant "Apostle to the Gentiles" effected a bridge between the faith of the Apostles and the Gentile, pagan world in the way in which such bridges are usually constructed – by a series of compromises. The Jewish Messiah was subtly converted into a universal saviour god in the tradition of the Egyptian Osiris and the Greek Dionysius. Even in the much-mutilated version that has come down to us of The Acts of the Apostles, the conflict between the two traditions is clearly defined. It is made to centre on the ritual act of circumcision as a requirement for admission to the Jerusalem-oriented Jewish sect. In reality, matters of deeper significance were at issue, in particular the human or divine nature of Jesus of Nazareth.

It seems reasonably clear now, drawing on ancient sources and modern scholarship, that the apostolic, which is to say, Jewish, concept of the relationship between God and Jesus was that the affiliation was purely symbolic. Jesus of Nazareth was a man and prophet who was adopted by God as his son at the moment of his baptism by St. John the Baptist. He became, because of his perfect life, like God, but not identical with him.

The Book of Acts and the letters of St. Paul would have us believe that this matter was settled in favour of St. Paul and his followers at the Council of Jerusalem. Such was not the case. The apostolic tradition of the human nature of Jesus continued to flourish, particularly among the Jewish Christians of Asia Minor, until the fourth century. It was not in fact until the first council of Nicaea, convened by Constantine the Great in 325 A.D. that this and other doctrines concerning the human and/or divine natures of the Christ were declared to be heretical.

If Quetzalcoatl and his comrades were Jewish Christians, following in the apostolic tradition, from which they were only half a century removed, the emphasis in their teaching would not have been on the divine nature of the Messiah. His life would not consequently have assumed the importance it did in the Gentile church; whereas the nature of God, the incomprehensible prime Spirit, expressed in all aspects of the natural world, including that emanation of Him who died on Calvary, would have been central to their faith.

Such an interpretation as this would account for virtually every peculiarity noted in the faith instituted by Quetzalcoatl of Teotihuacán in the second century A.D.

Chapter Thirteen

SINGERS OF SONGS

I, the singer, polished my noble new song like a shining emerald, I
arranged it like the voice of the *tzinitzcan* bird, I called to mind the
essence of poetry, I set it in order like the chant of the *zacuan* bird, I
mingled it with the beauty of the emerald, that I might make it appear
like a rose bursting its bud, so that I might rejoice the Cause of All.

   – An Otomi Song of the Mexicans. From Daniel G. Brinton, *Ancient
   Nahuatl Poetry.*

It has been pointed out by several writers that the art and literature of
the native civilizations of the Americas can be understood only in the
light of the pre-eminence of religion and religious symbolism in the
life of the people.

   There is much evidence to suggest that, in Mexico at least, the so-
called Archaic Period was, as Laurette Séjourné puts it, a "pre-religious
stage." That is to say, it was a stage in which magic was the predomi-
nant force, when the component parts of the human environment were
isolated entities, "having no inner communion with the rest." This was
the world of totems, of fertility cults, of shamanism and initiation
rites, from which many American tribes never broke free. Religion,
Mme Séjourné says, conceives "the various parts to be emanations from
an invisible whole," putting an end to multiplicity and fragmentation
and opening to its believers a vision of transcendence. This requires a
revelation of the wholeness of creation and of mankind's role in it.
"The true essence of every religious system," she says, "lies in the
revelation of an individual soul closely bound to the soul of the cos-
mos: it has to do, in other words, with making man divine."

   That such a revelation came to the high cultures of the Americas is
no longer in doubt; nor can the source of the revelation any longer be a
mystery:

As to the Nahuatl religion, this primordial revelation is expressed with great density and luminosity in the different myths of Quetzalcoatl, myths which fill most of the documents of Meso-american history.[1]

The vision of transcendence can only be expressed in language that transcends that of normal human usage. The most luminous form of human verbal expression is poetry. The Indians of the Americas have seldom been thought of as poets or singers of songs; the beat of the tom-tom and the savagery of the Sun Dance is about as near as the average person comes to a knowledge of native literature and song. The "inglorious Miltons" of aboriginal America were not so much mute as muffled. Yet, despite the iconoclastic depredations of the white conquerors and soul-savers, a respectable body of American literature has come down to us which even translation cannot deprive of dignity and grandeur.

The language in which these thoughts are written is reminiscent of the best which has been preserved for us from our own heritage of the ancient world. The relationship between man and the universe was expressed by members of the Omaha tribe in a hymn which evokes memories of the Benedicite, Omnia Opera:[2]

Ho! Ye Sun, Moon, Stars, all ye that move in the heavens, I bid you
hear me!
Into your midst has come a new life. Consent ye, I implore!
Make its path smooth, that it may reach the brow of the first hill! [3]

The appearance of the world at the dawn of creation, as recorded in the *Popul Vuh* of the Quiché-Maya, is as moving as the sophisticated language of the first chapter of the Book of Genesis:

Lo, all was suspense, all was calm and silent; all was motionless, all
was quiet, and wide was the immensity of the skies.
Lo, the first word and the first discourse.
There was not yet a man; not an animal; there were no birds nor
fish; there was no wood, no stone, no bog, no ravine, neither
vegetation nor marsh; only the sky existed.
The face of the earth was not yet to be seen; only the peaceful sea
and the expanse of the heavens.
Nothing was yet formed into a body; nothing was joined to another

121

thing; naught held itself poised; there was not a rustle, not a
sound beneath the sky.

There was naught that stood upright; there were only the quiet
waters of the sea, solitary within its bounds; for as yet naught
existed.

There were only immobility and silence in the darkness and in the
night.

Alone was the Creator, the Maker, Tepeu, the Lord, and Gucumatz,
the Plumed Serpent, those who engender, those who give being,
alone upon the waters like a growing light.[4]

Aside from the *Popul Vuh*, very little Mayan literature has survived.
The Nahuatl tribes of Mexico were more fortunate. In one instance
not only has the poetry survived but so also has the memory of the
poet. Nezahualcoyotl, king of Texcoco, lived from 1392 to 1472. He
was remembered as a great patron of the arts, particularly poetry. He
was also a devotee of the cult of Quetzalcoatl, whose pure faith he
attempted unsuccessfully to revive. He tried with equal lack of success
to stem the tide of human sacrifice demanded by the Aztec wargod,
Huitzilopochtli.

Nezahualcoyotl spent most of the first thirty years of his life in
poverty as he hid from the usurper of his rightful place, King Tezozomoc, who had murdered Nezahualcoyotl's father. During this
period much of his time was passed in fasting and prayer and in the
writing of "songs." Of the sixty poems with which he is credited, four
have come down to us in their entirety. In their style and content they
show us a gentle philosophical mind trying to cope with the eternal
mysteries of life and death and the vanity of human existence:

The fleeting pomps of the world are like the green willow trees,
which, aspiring to permanence, are consumed by a fire, fall before
the axe, are upturned by the wind, or are scarred and saddened by
age.

The grandeurs of life are like the flowers in colour and in fate; the
beauty of these remains so long as their chaste buds gather and
store the rich pearls of the dawn and saving it, drop it in liquid
dew; but scarcely has the Cause of All directed upon them the
full rays of the sun, when their beauty and glory fail, and the
brilliant gay colours which decked forth their pride wither and
fade.

The delicious realms of flowers count their dynasties by short periods; those which in the morning revel proudly in beauty and strength, by evening weep for the sad destruction of their thrones, and for the mishaps which drive them to loss, to poverty, to death and to the grave.

All things of earth have an end, and in the midst of the most joyous lives, the breath falters, they fall, they sink into the ground.

All the earth is a grave, and naught escapes it; nothing is so perfect that it does not fall and disappear.

The rivers, brooks, fountains and waters flow on, and never return to their joyous beginnings; they hasten on to the vast realms of Tlaloc, and the wider they spread between their marges the more rapidly do they mold their own sepulchral urns.

That which was yesterday is not today; and let not that which is today trust to live tomorrow.[5]

One is reminded strongly in this passage of that other lamentation, that biblical Thanatopsis, the Book of Ecclesiastes:

If a man live many years, and rejoice in them all; yet let him remember the days of darkness; for they shall be many. All that cometh is vanity.[6]

The unknown Jewish lecturer of 200 B.C. wrought his melancholic wisdom in an era of social corruption and oppression. Nezahualcoyotl's thoughts on death were forged in a like cauldron of deceit, treason, and corruption, at a time when the Aztec state had made human sacrifice an instrument of political expediency rather than a religious necessity, as it had earlier been considered to be.

The caverns of the earth are filled with pestilential dust which once was the bones, the flesh, the bodies of great ones who sat upon thrones, deciding causes, ruling assemblies, governing armies, conquering provinces, possessing treasures, tearing down temples, flattering themselves with pride, majesty, fortune, praise and dominion.

These glories have passed like the dark smoke thrown out by the fires of Popocatepetl, leaving no monuments but the rude skins on which they are written.

Ha! Ha! Were I to introduce you into the obscure bowels of this temple, and were to ask you which of these bones were those of the powerful Acholchiuhtlanextin, first chief of the ancient Toltecs; of Necazecmitl, devout worshipper of the gods; if I inquire where is the peerless beauty of the glorious empress Xiuhtzal, where the peaceable Topiltzin, last monarch of the hapless land of Tulan; if I ask you where are the sacred ashes of our first father Xolotl; those of the bounteous Nopal; those of the generous Tlotzin; or even the still warm cinders of my glorious and immortal, though unhappy and luckless father Ixtlilxochitl; if I continued thus questioning about all our august ancestors, what would you reply?

The same that I reply – I know not, I know not; for first and last are confounded in the common clay.

What was their fate shall be ours, and of all who follow us.

Or as the Jewish writer said, more succinctly, men, like animals, "all go unto one place; all are of the dust and all turn to dust again." [7]

There is one basic difference, however, between the philosophies of Nezahualcoyotl and the writer of Ecclesiastes. The Jewish writer's cynicism is absolute. There is no dawn in his darkness. "Fear God and keep his commandments," he says in a rather tendentious afterthought, "for this is the whole duty of man." The Mexican writer, on the other hand, ends his song on a note of eternal hope, a luminous glimpse of heaven, a hint of the high purpose of the Cause of All.

Unconquered princes, warlike chieftains, let us seek, let us sigh for the heaven, for there all is eternal, and nothing is corruptible.

The darkness of the sepulchre is but the strengthening couch for the glorious sun, and the obscurity of the night but serves to reveal the brilliancy of the stars.

No one has power to alter these heavenly lights, for they serve to display the greatness of their Creator, and as our eyes see them now, so saw them our earliest ancestors, and so shall see them our latest posterity.

The difference between Ecclesiastes and the Song of Nezahualcoyotl is precisely the difference between the Old Testament and the New; between a God-burdened people and a God-delivered people; between a nation of wayfarers walking a dark road beginning nowhere and ending nowhere and a nation walking in the light of a high and holy hope.

When it is again considered how many years and how many shattered empires lay between the King of Texcoco and the initial teachings of Quetzalcoatl, the power of that first revelation may faintly be glimpsed.

Chapter Fourteen

ART AND THE SOUL

In the Gothic style, beauty is not the end of artistic creation. It mobilizes all its creative energies to give expression to metaphysical-religious experience. What we recognize as beauty we place there ourselves. . . . It seems to me that this can be applied without reservation to the art of ancient Mexico, for neither does pre-Cortesian man create art for art's sake.

– Paul Westheim, *The Art of Ancient Mexico.*

The art of the natives of pre-Columbian America did not at first find favour with Europeans. It was considered "grotesque," "barbaric," "primitive." Grotesque and barbaric it may have appeared – and still does appear – to those reared to respect Old World standards of beauty. Primitive it most certainly is not.

Paul Westheim's illuminating study on Mexican art, from which I have quoted at the head of this chapter, makes it quite clear that pre-Columbian art was directed to a totally different purpose from that of ancient Greek art, for instance. It was not beauty the American artist sought, but spirituality. Westheim quite properly draws a parallel with Gothic art, the purpose of which was the same.

We are confronted everywhere in the Americas by images of strange people, animals, and birds performing incomprehensible acts; by florid scenes, extravagantly embellished. We see Mayan stelae with every square inch of space jammed with apparently meaningless curlicues and decorations like a Victorian title-page or the ancient Irish Book of Kells. We accept the book-plate and the Irish manuscript because they both happen to fall within the stream of our racial and historical consciousness – but for the art of Teotihuacán, of Palenque, and of Tiahuanaco we have no artistic vocabulary.

Christianity, like most religions, has always leaned heavily on symbolism. Without knowledge of the background, many of the symbols used in Christian art would be as meaningless as some of the as-yet undeciphered Mayan hieroglyphs. One need only mention a few examples – the nails of the Crucifixion, the pincers of St. Agatha, the rope of Judas, the balance of the Archangel Michael, the wheel of Ezekiel, the key of St. Peter, the crutch of St. Anthony and the trefoil of the Holy Trinity. If it were not for biblical texts and the vast body of church tradition, the special meaning of these objects would be totally lost on us and the stained glass windows in tens of thousands of churches would appear grotesque, barbaric, and baffling – as indeed many of them do.

American native art was symbolic. The symbolism was religious. This fact must be understood before anything at all can be made of it. As so often happens with religious symbolism the forms became fixed and rigid, resistant to alteration and change. What change took place over the centuries was towards "purification" – a reduction of unnecessary external attributes of the symbolic object and a greater concentration on its spiritual content. In much the same way, the great Russian painter, Wasilly Kandinsky, refined his perception of the world from the impressionistic *The Blue Rider* (1903) to the pure form and colour of such later works as *A Conglomerate* (1943) seeking always the truth that reveals "the spiritual core beneath merely superficial physical existence." [1]

To achieve this subjection of the external to the internal and eternal, the native American artists, especially in Middle America, tended to favour monumental forms, just as did the builders of the Gothic cathedrals in Europe and of the pyramids in ancient Egypt. The attributes of God in nature were shown to be awesome, even horrendous. No one who sees the great mass of the image of Tlaloc, the rain god, at the entrance to the National Museum of Anthropology in Mexico City can fail to be impressed by this ugly, blocky, misshapen but immensely powerful representation of a natural force.[2]

The American natives worshipped God, not beauty. To quote Paul Westheim again:

An aesthetic study of Mesoamerican art must start from the integral subjection to religion and the peculiar nature of this religiosity, and it must be remembered that such subjection was not considered a restriction, but the true end of artistic goals . . . . God is not new or interesting; God is old and eternal. To give plastic expression to this

127

old, traditional and sacred representation of the divine is the mission of art. If our desire for an individual artistic style, for an individual personality and mode of expression, is satisfied only slightly if at all by pre-Columbian art, it is precisely because the function of this art was to give the masses of the faithful the form that embodied age-old symbols which, as transformations of their devotion, were above the individual, expressive, visionary, valid for all and comprehensible to all.[3]

It was not always so. The earliest art of the Americas is of quite another sort. To begin with, the work of the artists, sculptors and potters of the so-called pre-Classic period was remarkably homogeneous throughout the areas where the high cultures later developed. Communication has been shown to have existed between Middle America and the Peruvian coast for a few centuries beginning about 800 B.C.

The widespread styles of this period are in marked contrast to the heavy religiosity of later eras. The art of the pre-Classic is gay, joyous, carefree – and naturalistic. The most characteristic artifacts of this early time are little doll-like clay figurines found literally by the thousands at ancient sites in Mexico. They often represent nude women. The earliest specimens are crudely made, with a ball of clay serving as the pupil of the eye, small rolls of clay representing the arms and legs and a few scratched incisions for the fingers and toes. On the other hand, great care is shown in reproducing the often elaborate hairdos and ornaments in which the ladies obviously took great pride. Later more sophisticated models often had articulated arms and legs.

Archaeologists and ethnologists, who, like ministers of religion, are always keen to read symbolic meanings into the minutiae of civilized societies, at first assumed the naked ladies to be fertility fetishes. This theory has now been abandoned. Whether this was because of the coiffures or for some other reason, I do not know, nor do I know what theory if any has replaced the abandoned hypothesis. I suppose it would be considered simplistic to suggest that they were merely children's toys.

At any rate the figurines and other examples of pre-Classic art show a determined concentration on the material rather than on the spiritual aspects of living. As the late Miguel Covarrubias said in reference to one of the most important pre-Classic sites in Mexico: "Evidently religious symbolism did not exist for the people of Tlatilco." What

The young Quetzalcoatl. Note the
European features, the neatly-trimmed
beard, the prominent nose and large
eyes. A low-relief carving on the back
of a slate mirror from Vera Cruz,
Mexico.

Clay head (far left) found at Tres Zapotes, Mexico. Found in same general area as the young Quetzalcoatl on previous page.

The mature Quetzalcoatl (left). Jade image from the tomb of the high priest at Palenque.

The gentle old Bochica (below) of the Mochica. Pottery jar from North Peru, second century A.D.

Huehuetéotl (right), the "old god," the god of fire. Teotihuacán, second century A.D.

A terracotta portrait head (left) of a bearded white man from the Gulf Coast of Mexico, where many portrait images of European types have been found (before 600 A.D.).

A powerful stone sculpture (right) popularly known as "The Wrestler." Credited to the Olmec culture of the Gulf Coast; probably about the beginning of the Christian era.

A bold Old World face (below) on the front of an incense burner from the Maya zone near Chimaltenango, Guatemala. Similar incense burners are found in Vera Cruz, Mexico, *c.* 300 A.D.

Stele (right) from Tepatlazco, Vera Cruz, Mexico, (c. 600 A.D.). An official adjusts the protective pads around the hips of a man about to take part in the sacred ball game. The player's beard is false. The beard and moustache of the official appear to be natural.

The "Roman" head (opposite page) excavated from the pyramid at Calixtlahuaca, Mexico, by Juan Garcia Payon, is said to be of European manufacture and to date to the second century A.D..

A stucco portrait head (below) of a European type with beard, moustache and braided headgear. From the Maya zone, State of Tabasco, Mexico. Attributed to the pre-Classic period (600 B.C.-300 A.D.).

This low-relief sculpture from the Temple of Kukulcan, at Chichén Itzá, Yucatan, Mexico, may represent the Toltec prince who established his rule over the Maya in the tenth or eleventh century A.D.

An extremely striking terracotta portrait of a bearded and moustached man of obviously European features from Jaina, Campeche, Mexico. Attributed to the late Classic period, that is, after 1000 A.D. Note the similarity of the head-dresses in both portraits.

Among the racial types illustrated by the terracotta portraits found in great numbers throughout Mexico, many are negroid in appearance. These two are of comparatively late date – around 1000 A.D.

Five small terracotta heads from Teotihuacán, Mexico. The terracottas from the earliest period were made by hand; the later figures were turned out from moulds in enormous quantities.

The terracotta art of the Mexican State of Vera Cruz presents an astonishing variety of racial types. This head, termed a very rare example by Alexander von Wuthenau, is attributed to the Totonac culture (300-600 A.D.).

A rare example of a Semitic type from Western Mexico, where the legend of Quetzalcoatl was scarcely known until the time of the Aztecs.

A dignified European face from Palenque, the city said to have been founded by Votan. Pre-classic Maya; second or third century A.D.

A bearded and moustached "soldier" (above) of the Totonac culture of the Gulf Coast of Mexico.

An elephant-like figure (above) with a beak instead of a trunk. Totonac culture.

A toy dog with wheels (below), from Tres Zapotes, Vera Cruz. Classic period (300-600 A.D.)

A "demonic lion" (right) similar to artifacts noted by Robert Heine-Geldern and to models found in India.

Jewish coin of the revolution of Simon Bar Kokhba (132-135 A.D.), found in Kentucky.

Inscription found in a burial mound at Bat Creek, Tennessee, by an expedition from the Smithsonian Institution.

Doorway to a ruined temple (right) at Chichén Itzá, Yucatan. Atlantean figures support a stone lintel on which a date in the Mayan hieroglyphs has been carved corresponding to the seventh century in the Christian calendar.

The strange circular temple (below) of Quetzalcoatl in his guise as Ehécatl, "the god of the winds," at Calixtlahuaca, Mexico. This is where the little head, said to be of European manufacture, was found in 1938 by Juan Garcia Payon.

Grey-blue jade mask of the Olmec
culture, termed "America's first
civilization." From Las Bocas, Puebla,
Mexico, middle pre-Classic period
(1000-600 B.C.).

was true of Tlatilco, an archaeological site in the Valley of Mexico west of Mexico City, was equally true of pre-Classic culture wherever it is found.

What caused the change and when and where did it occur? Of some peculiar specimens of the clay figurines dating to late in this particular era, Paul Westheim wrote:

> Occasionally two-headed figures are found or figures with only one head and two faces. In this latter case there are three eyes, the centre one shared by both faces. A sculptural type that has been found in Tlatilco and in some other regions is a kind of mask with two entirely different halves; one half has characteristically represented human features: the eye, the nose, the tongue that appears between the lips, and wrinkles above the eye and mouth. The other part is half a skull, with an empty eye socket. It is not at all unlikely that this is a symbol – the first – of the dualism that governs the Mexican theogony.

Suddenly the meaning of life – and death – has changed. A woman's coiffure is now not as important as her soul. The children's toys take on a sombre dichotomy.

What had happened?

Quetzalcoatl had arrived at Teotihuacán.

The appearance of the new artifacts can be dated approximately at the end of the pre-Classic period – 100 A.D. to 200 A.D. The old, carefree, joyous and gay art of pre-Columbian America had disappeared for all time – except in one area. That area was Western Mexico. The art of Michoacan and Guerrero, of Colima, Jalisco and Nayarit, is totally different from that of the rest of Middle America. The artistic language of the ancient peoples of these areas descends directly from the plastic idiom of the pre-Classic period. Westheim effectively describes the difference:

> While the art of Teotihuacán, the Toltecs, Aztecs and Zapotecs has an essentially religious orientation and one subject – the representation of the divinities and of the cosmic happenings – a worldly attitude predominates in Western Mexico. In the ceramics of this culture, of which innumerable examples are preserved, it seems that the gods did not exist. What it represents are men and women, animals and fruit. A surprising phenomenon is the numerous

"genre scenes." There are warriors with their arms; slings, wooden swords, clubs and axes. Ballplayers in their special outfit. Chiefs, musicians, acrobats, men and women dancers. Women nursing their children, stripping ears of corn, grinding maize, making tortillas, combing their own hair or that of another woman. Love scenes. Chiefs borne on litters by four bearers; often their wives sit close to them and sometimes a dog accompanies them. Others are seated on stools protected, in some cases, by canopies. Groups of dancers, dancing around the musicians, to the sound of drums and tambourines. Domestic scenes: the rectangular house with its steep roof painted in a rich ornamentation; the husband, wife and children squat in the entry. Animals of all kinds – dogs, monkeys (there is a figure of a monkey yawning with his mouth wide open), turtles, ducks, herons, parakeets, spiders, fish, sharks . . . . There are the most diverse objects: arms, musical instruments, fans, obsidian mirrors. The characteristics notable in the human figures are the often extravagant headdress and the finely executed body painting that indicated social standing. Profane art, which delights in the description of daily life and seems to ignore what for Teotihuacán and the whole Nahua world was the only thing worthy of being represented: the supra-earthly and the transcendental.

There are no metaphysical words in the language of the people of Western Mexico, whom the Spaniards called collectively the Tarascans.

Why? While the Spanish friars found evidence of the worship of certain gods, many of whom could be identified with similar deities in other parts of Mexico, they were all late importations. There had been little continuous contact or influence with other parts of Middle America until the period of Aztec domination.

There was no native Tarascan legend about a bearded white stranger.

Quetzalcoatl did not get to Western Mexico.

PART IV

WAYS AND MEANS

Chapter Fifteen

VESSELS AND DESTINATIONS

Oskar Peschel, one of the founders of modern geography, once said that since time immemorial "the two banks of the Atlantic Valley announced their presence to one another."

— Paul Herrmann, *Conquest by Man.*

1

The *Santa Maria*, flagship of Christopher Columbus' transatlantic expedition in 1492, was a vessel of eighty tons. The two caravels that accompanied her, the *Nina* and the *Pinta*, were smaller — sixty tons each. Henry Hudson's *Half Moon* which carried her master's name deep into the heart of the North American continent, the *Mayflower*, which took the New England pilgrims to their landing at Plymouth Rock, and the *Nonsuch*, which established the presence of English merchant power in Hudson Bay, were all smaller than many private yachts which today ply the inland lakes and rivers of the New World.

Yet, while we marvel at the temerity of captains and crews who dared the wastes of North Atlantic waters in such tiny vessels, we are accustomed to deny the possibility of such voyages in the much larger ships of the great nations of the ancient world. The ship which carried St. Paul from Asia Minor to Rome had a total passenger and crew list of 276 persons.[1] Josephus, the Jewish historian, speaks of a ship with a passenger list of 600 which also carried cargo. Lucian writes of a grain ship running out of Alexandria which had a displacement of more than 2,000 tons. An earlier vessel, an armoured ship of King Ptolemy Philopator, was said to be 426 feet long and of 6,500 tons burden. The ships that brought the liberated Egyptian obelisks to Rome also carried wheat and were in the order of 2,500 tons.

Such large ships were, of course, exceptional. The coastal trading

133

ships were much smaller. It has been estimated that the vessels which carried on the bulk of Mediterranean shipping had displacements of 200 to 400 tons. Even these would have been from three to five times as large as Columbus' flagship.

The Mediterranean Sea is not always the placid blue lake of the travel agents' brochures. St. Paul's vivid account of the perils of the sea encountered on his journey to Rome makes hair-raising reading. Ships capable of making such voyages as these were surely equally capable of crossing the Atlantic from east to west. It is true that the vessels of the ancient world were not as manoeuvrable as the European ships of the fifteenth and sixteenth centuries. It is not true, as has been so often stated, that they could not tack into the wind. J.V. Luce is the most recent author to scotch this canard. In *The Quest for America* (New York: 1971) he quotes from Aristotle and Virgil to prove that the ancients were familiar with this procedure from at least the fourth century B.C.

It has been shown that there was a brisk trade between Rome and India. These voyages required the ships to run before the monsoons on the outward journey across the open sea for periods of up to forty days. The homeward journey, made with a following northeast wind, usually took even longer. The vessels that made these journeys were probably of comparable size with the larger Mediterranean trading and passenger ships.

It has been demonstrated again and again in the past century that vessels as small as rowboats and as clumsy as reed rafts are capable of making transatlantic voyages from east to west; and a few have proved that the normally more difficult west-east crossing can also be made in very small craft.

In the face of proven trade between centres far distant from one another, across open sea, the size of the vessels employed, and the obvious qualities of seamanship required to complete such voyages, it is ridiculous to claim that the ships and mariners of the ancient world were incapable of crossing the Atlantic and making a successful landfall on the western shores of the Ocean Sea.

Thor Heyerdahl, the intrepid scholar who has crossed both the Atlantic and Pacific oceans in vessels designed after ancient European and American craft, has several times over earned the right to be considered the authority on the feasibility of such voyages and the means by which they might have been accomplished. He has pointed out many times that wind and water currents in the Atlantic form invisible "conveyor belts" linking Europe and America. He cites three such conveyors – two from east to west, and one from west to east. The northern route from Europe to America is that followed by the Norse settlers of Newfoundland in the eleventh century A.D. The southern and easier route is the one Columbus took. The departure route follows the Gulf Stream. Heyerdahl dismisses this as a means of ancient contact because "it would be inhospitable to tropically acclimatized natives of Central America who would be little prepared to survive the long northbound drift into the cold North Atlantic." He does not mention, or perhaps he has not considered, the possibility that such hardships would pose no insuperable obstacles to Mediterranean mariners undertaking a *return* voyage from North America to Europe.

2

Eratosthenes (275-195 B.C.), one of the greatest minds of the world of classical antiquity, capped his scientific career by discovering and applying the mathematical concept of the measurement of the earth's surface by degrees of a circle. In one of the most important experiments ever carried out, he measured the number of degrees between Alexandria, in Egypt and Syene (the modern Aswan). On the basis of his findings he calculated that the continent of the Old World (Europe and Asia) occupied about one third of the circumference of the globe of the earth. The distance, therefore, between the coast of Spain and the eastern Asiatic coast was approximately 240 degrees of longitude. This remarkable calculation is strikingly close to the true figure. He concluded:

> Only that area of the earth in which we ourselves live and which is known to us is called by us *Oikoumene*, inhabited world. But there may well be another, or even several more inhabited continents in the temperate zone.

While Eratosthenes' science did not have the lasting influence that it truly deserved, his findings were not particularly alien to the ancient world. From very early times the Greeks had considered the inhabited world, the *Oikoumene*, to be a disc surrounded by the waters of *Okeanos*, the world river. If *Okeanos* was a river, it was logical to assume that there was another shore opposite the *Oikoumene*.

The afterworld, the world beyond the grave, was placed by all the ancient peoples of the Mediterranean basin, beginning with the Egyptians, on that mysterious other shore or the islands off its coast. It was in the west, in the land beyond the sunset, that the Kingdom of the Dead lay. The Blessed Isles, Elysium, were on that other shore. At the end of life "the immortals will send you to the Elysian plain at the world's end . . . in the land where living is made easiest for mankind, where no snow falls, no strong winds blow and there is never any rain, but day after day the West Wind's tuneful breeze comes in from Ocean to refresh its folk."

By the time of Eratosthenes, Mediterranean mariners had greatly expanded European knowledge of the *Oikoumene*. Twice within a century expeditions set out to circumnavigate Africa. The first, under Egyptian auspices but employing Phoenician ships and sailors, actually completed a voyage around Africa from east to west, from the Red Sea clockwise. Some 200 years later this adventure was chronicled somewhat sceptically by Herodotus the Greek historian (485-425 B.C.):

> As for Libya [Africa] we know it to be washed on all sides by the sea, except where it is attached to Asia. The discovery was first made by Necho the Egyptian king who . . . sent to sea a number of ships manned by Phoenicians, with orders to make for the Pillars of Hercules, and to return to Egypt through them and through the Mediterranean. The Phoenicians took their departure from Egypt by way of the Erythraean Sea and so sailed into the Southern Ocean. When autumn came they went ashore, wherever they might happen to be, and having sown a tract of land with corn, waited until the grain was fit to be cut. Having reaped it, they again set sail; and thus it came to pass that two whole years went by, and it was not until the third year that they doubled the Pillars of Hercules and made good their voyage home. On their return they declared (I for my part do not believe them, but perhaps others may) that in sailing round Libya they got the sun on their right hand. In this way was the extent of Libya first discovered.

The very thing that caused Herodotus to doubt the account is precisely the fact that assures us of its authenticity. For ships sailing south of the equator the sun does indeed appear north of the zenith – "they got the sun on their right hand."

The name of the commander of this extraordinarily daring expedition is not recorded – only that of his royal patron. This gives us an approximate date for the accomplishment. Necho II, third pharaoh of the 26th (Saite) dynasty, ruled Egypt from 609 to 593 B.C.

Nearly a century later a second Phoenician expedition attempted to circumnavigate Africa in the opposite direction from west to east, from the Pillars of Hercules to the Red Sea. This was a vastly more difficult undertaking and the farthest south they got was probably the coast of Sierra Leone in West Africa, although this point is still being disputed. This second adventure was wholly Phoenician. The commander was Hanno, of Carthage, the great Phoenician colony which for a century challenged Rome for supremacy in the Mediterranean. Through the curiosity of a Greek tourist Hanno's log, to which the name *periplus* was applied in the Greek, has survived to our day. Hanno had posted the account of his voyage in the temple of Baal at Carthage by way of a thank-offering. There it was observed by a visiting Greek who copied it. It was subsequently cited in a work of the third century B.C. attributed to Aristotle. It is one of the very few accounts of Phoenician navigation to come down to us. The Phoenician merchant-mariners jealously guarded their navigational knowledge from all competitors.

According to the Periplus of Hanno his expedition was intended to establish colonies on the west coast of Libya (Africa). He had command of sixty ships of fifty oars each, carrying 30,000 colonists. While doubts have been expressed about the reported number of men and women taking part, the other details of the voyage are today widely accepted as being completely authentic.

These two voyages alone are enough to account for the almost legendary reputation of the Phoenician seafarers from their day to ours. Further accounts make it clear that their vessels traded in tin with the Cornish coast of England and in amber with the peoples of the North Sea and the Baltic coast. Their ships skirted the shores of Scotland and ranged north as far as Iceland.

Seamen who could make such remarkable journeys were certainly capable of extending their range across the milder reaches of the Atlantic. Indeed, Phoenician inscriptions have been reported found in the Canary Islands and a mass of Carthaginian coins on the island of Corvo in the Azores.

The Phoenicians were not the only peoples of the Eastern Mediterranean to possess seamanship to a high degree. Dr. Cyrus H. Gordon and others have pointed out that the Israelites were partners with the Phoenicians in merchant marine activity from the time of King Solomon in the tenth century B.C. until well down into the Roman imperial period. At Jaffa (Biblical Joppa) during the First Jewish Rebellion (66-70 A.D.), Roman naval forces won a victory over a large Jewish fleet; its size may be judged by Josephus' statement that the bodies of 4,200 drowned Jews were counted after the battle. Any objective study of Jewish history will reveal the fallacy of the often repeated comment that the Israelites were "the least nautical nation of antiquity."

The Romans could not call the Mediterranean *Mare Nostrum* until they had learned the art of seamanship from their rivals and enemies. They perfected that art as a military weapon; their rivals, the Phoenicians and Jews, had employed it principally as a tool of trade. Generals and admirals are not interested in exploration and discovery, but in conquest. Merchants are continually seeking for new markets, new sources of raw materials. The beginning of the era of Roman rule of the sea effectively marked the end of the great ancient period of exploration and discovery.

None of their successors in the ancient world – certainly not mighty Rome – ever equalled the peoples of the Palestinian coast in their navigational knowledge of the sea-lanes of the northern hemisphere. What they learned they never fully revealed; it comes down to us in tantalizing dribs and drabs. However, enough has survived to make it reasonably certain that many among the population of seafarers in the eastern end of the Mediterranean knew of the existence of a great island or continent westward on the Atlantic. Others had guessed at the existence of such a land mass.

Even a cursory study of the winds and the water currents of the Atlantic makes it obvious that flotsam and jetsam must have many times drifted from one shore to the other of *Okeanos*. The northeast trade winds and the North Equatorial Current flowing from Spain to the New World; the Gulf Stream and the prevailing westerlies leading from North America to Europe – these provide, as Thor Heyerdahl has pointed out, a conveyor belt between the continents of the eastern and western hemispheres.

Strange plants, reeds, pieces of wood and bamboo – the two latter sometimes carved with stone tools – had been reported washed up on the shores of Europe from early times. Claudius Ptolemaeus, a Greek geographer of the second century A.D., listed a number of these finds and gave his opinion that they came from Asia.

It was another Greek geographer, Pausanias, who around 150 A.D. stated baldly that far west of the Ocean there lay a group of islands whose inhabitants were red-haired and wore horses' tails on their flanks. Like many of the ancient writers, Pausanias does not bother to quote an authority for this astonishing statement. A Roman writer, Pomponius Mela, a native of Spain, was much more helpful. In his magnum opus, *De Choregraphia*, written between 40 and 44 A.D., he quotes the Roman historian Cornelius Nepos, who in turn received his information from Q. Metellus Celer, who said that when he was pro-consul in Gaul in 62 B.C. "several Indians were presented to him as a gift by the king of the Suevans. On inquiring where these men had come from, he was told that they had come from the Indian seas, having been carried by high winds across the intervening seas and finally cast up on the shores of Germany."

As an example of the peculiar kind of negative thinking that afflicts scholars in this field, their reaction to the story of Quintus Metellus Celer is typical. They are impressed by this account. In spite of Thor Heyerdahl's conclusion concerning the improbability of a native American voyage across the cold North Atlantic, they give a fair amount of weight to this evidence. Yet many of the same men will dismiss out of hand the authority of the legend of Quetzalcoatl which postulates a voyage by the opposite, much easier route.

Objectively, both the story of Quintus Metellus Celer and the Quetzalcoatl legend depend on hearsay evidence. The Roman account was reported at third- or possibly even fourth-hand (from Quintus Metellus Celer to Cornelius Nepos to Pomponius Mela and, later still, to Pliny).

Yet one account is accepted, the other rejected. Why? The answer is simple, but psychologically deep-seated. The American legend was transmitted *orally* by *non-Europeans* ; the Celer story was *written down* by *Europeans*. Mankind is not yet far removed from his primitive begin-nings; whatever is out of the mainstream of the culture of his tribe, nation, or civilization is "barbarian" and suspect. To the ancient Greeks, all non-Greeks were barbarians; to Western man all that is not provably of Greek or Roman origin is likewise barbarian and hence untrustworthy. The same, of course, was true of the American natives; the Maya looked upon themselves as "true men" – all others were shadow men and potentially inimical. And yet the Aztecs and the Incas trusted Cortés and Pizarro out of reverence for the memory of the great high priest, Quetzalcoatl.

While the story told by the proconsul of Gaul is probably the most dramatic evidence to come from the ancient world, scores of other writers record instances that reveal a practical if scanty knowledge of the world beyond the ocean. Seneca (5 B.C. –65 A.D.) tells of a vessel which from its description was a North American Indian canoe with a crew of dead, red-skinned men. Plutarch (46-120 A.D.) describes a group of islands in the latitude of Britain beyond which stretches a great continent. These islands, he said, are unusual because for thirty days they have unbroken sunshine. During the night the sun is invisible for about an hour, but it does not become quite dark – the western sky glows with a luminous twilight. This account of conditions near the Arctic Circle cannot possibly be attributed to pure imagination.[2]

When to these tantalizing scraps of information we add that the Canary Islands and the Azores – those stepping stones of the Atlantic – were known to the ancient mariners long before the birth of Christ, and that the northeast trade winds begin just to the west of Cape Verde with a strength sufficient to propel even the crudest vessel a great way out – then it becomes obvious that the two banks of the Atlantic valley had not only announced their presence to one another, as Oskar Peschel wrote, but that they had recognized one another.

I think it must be noted, in connection with this brief summary, that the paucity of reliable information about transatlantic voyages at an early date is not necessarily due to a lack of knowledge on the part of the ancients. It must be remembered that history, which is more often a chronicle of wars and disasters than of peacetime achievement, has seen fit to bequeath us only a fraction of the books that were written.

PART V

WHO WAS
QUETZALCOATL?

Chapter Sixteen

THE NEW WORLD HERO

Many Indians of discretion said they had heard from their ancestors that certain people who had come from the east had settled that land. God had freed them from other peoples by opening a road for them through the sea.

— Antonio de Herrera, *Historia General.*

1

The enigma of Quetzalcoatl may forever remain unresolved. However, from the evidence so far presented one may safely arrive at certain broad conclusions:

1. The legend relates the story of a real person who was deified only after his death. He was a stranger to the peoples he visited and influenced. He was different from them in appearance. He wore a beard, a great rarity among the American natives. He is sometimes described as being "white" and frequently as wearing "long, flowing robes." He came from the east across the sea, according to the Middle-American versions of the legend. There are no specific references to his age in the Quetzalcoatl story. As Itzamna, in Yucatan, and as Bochica in South America, he is represented as an old man.

2. Archaeology tends to strengthen the evidence adduced from the legend. Hundreds of terracotta figurines found throughout Mexico portray persons of non-Indian appearance. The most common racial type shown can be identified as Semitic. These figurines are dated to the first three centuries of the Christian era. In addition, a significant group of portrait heads appear to illustrate the same individual as seen by the artists at different stages of his life from young manhood to extreme old age. I have identified this individual as the prototypal Quetzalcoatl. In the same area from which these influences radiate, a small figurine has been found which some European authorities have identified as a

common Mediterranean type of the second century A.D. Finally, a plaque bearing a Hebrew inscription and a number of coins dated to the Jewish rebellion of 132-135 A.D. have been found at sites in the states of Kentucky and Tennessee in the United States of America.

3. The evidence of native art, literature, and religion further reinforce the legend. It is apparent that at some stage in the first three Christian centuries a striking change took place in religious thinking over a very great area of Central and South America, with a consequent influence on art and literature. This change took the form of a strong trend towards monotheistic beliefs. In Mexico it was associated from a very early period with the cult of Quetzalcoatl and the great centre of Teotihuacán. The Middle-American myths of Creation and the Flood bear strong resemblances to the Hebrew accounts. Nevertheless, there are many indications that this new faith had embedded in it elements resembling early Christian practices and beliefs. For this reason I have speculated that the newcomers may have been Jewish Christians, members of the original apostolic community dispersed following the Roman capture and destruction of Jerusalem in 70 A.D.

There is no foreseeable end to the amount of speculation that this strange historical mystery has fostered now for more than 400 years. It may one day fall out as Tennyson wrote –

> The golden guess
> Is morning star to the full round of truth.

It would please me if mine should prove to be the "golden guess." Guess, however, it must remain until incontrovertible proof is presented either for or against it.

Speculation must begin with a discussion of the possibility of transatlantic sea contact between Europe and the Americas in the second Christian century.

2

The prototypal legend is quite specific about the direction from which the traveller came – over the seas from the east. Regional versions of the legend – in South America, for instance – cite points of origin which are compatible with a first landing somewhere in Middle America.

The archaeological record provides further evidence in that Middle

America has produced by far the greatest concentration of artifactual evidence of an intrusive nature, including at least two articles of European manufacture, as well as wheeled toys of a type unique in the Americas.

All these factors point to a European origin for the original Quetzalcoatl. The possibility of a transatlantic voyage can no longer be disputed; there were ships and sailors in the ancient world perfectly capable of completing such a voyage with a living crew.

When we attempt to identify these voyagers, by place of origin, racial type and occupation, we step into the world of the unknown. It is reasonably certain that the original names of the wayfarers may never be known. I must employ a cautious "may" since one cannot be sure what the soil of Middle and South America will yet reveal. In Mexico alone, at this writing, there are more than 12,000 listed archaeological sites. Of these less than 200 have been even partially excavated and a mere handful of this group have been extensively worked on. Even at the great city of Teotihuacán, where excavations have been carried on almost continuously since 1905, the work is far from complete. Tomorrow or next year or ten years from now, one of these 12,000 sites may yield conclusive proof of the theory advanced in this book or of a theory yet unformed.

The names of Quetzalcoatl and his comrades may be gone forever, but the facial features of two members of the party can be seen in the portrait images made by the artists of their adopted people. In the little clay heads found at Tres Zapotes and other Gulf Coast sites; in the image of the "old god," Huehueteotl, in the image found in the tomb of the high priest at Palenque, in the Mayan glyph representing Itzamna, in the protrait pottery jugs of the Mochica, Quetzalcoatl is clearly depicted through at least five of the "seven ages of man." The blocky Rio Balsas head and the Olmec and Mayan figurines of "The Wrestler" give us, I think, an adequate portrayal of one of Quetzalcoatl's friends.

I have said that the portraits which I have identified as those of Quetzalcoatl convey the impression of the Semitic type. The generous nose and the large eyes are major contributors to this feeling. Others – notably Alexander von Wuthenau – have shared this feeling. Nor is this by any means a subjective interpretation of the evidence. The most objective analysis of these striking figures is bound to result in the same conclusion. No one who has studied with any degree of care these obvious portraits can be fobbed off with academic double-talk about Indian "stylistic abstractions."

From these considerations, as well as from other data already discussed, a place of origin for Quetzalcoatl and his comrades somewhere in the Eastern Mediterranean is a reasonable speculation.

This impression is heightened by the legendary description of the dress worn by the strangers. The legends are reasonably consistent on this point. The newcomers wore "long, flowing robes," sufficiently striking among the lightly-clad Americans to win them the title of "Petticoated Ones" among the Tzendals of Middle America. "Long, flowing robes" – if this is an accurate translation of the native tradition – would be more descriptive of the common costume among the Jewish residents of the cities of Palestine and Asia Minor at the time of Christ than it would be of such Roman wear as the toga, which was not so much a robe as a drape.

Finally, the most telling piece of evidence pointing to a place of origin is to be found in the nature of the religion and religious practices that the newcomers brought. There is no hint in it of the polytheistic practices of the Roman Empire: no mystery cult, no emperor worship. Rather it is so strongly monotheistic, so powerfully God-centred, so symbolically oriented as to point unequivocally to the cradle of Old World monotheism, Jewry. At the same time the liturgical practices said to have stemmed from this contact are not at all similar to those of the Temple of Jerusalem. In their prayers they resemble rather the simpler worship of the synagogue, and in their rites those of that schismatic Jewish sect which followed the teachings of John the Baptist and Jesus of Nazareth. In fact, only from this latter source could possibly have come that constellation of worship rites which included baptism, confession, absolution, penance, a Eucharistic meal, and a hope of eternal life.

If these assumptions are correct then we must look for a community where the old covenant of God with the Hebrews was reinforced and rendered ecstatic by the overlay of a Messianic revelation by a prophet of God.

This can only refer to a group of Jewish Christians – members of that scattered community which under the leadership of James, the brother of Jesus, resisted the Pauline method of extending the Gospel to the Gentile world.[1] The Book of the Acts of the Apostles, written by St. Luke, clearly defines this dispute which was based ostensibly on the issue of circumcision as a necessary element for initiation into the sect, but in reality on the much more basic issue of the human or divine nature of the Messiah. (I have dealt with this aspect of the subject previously in the chapter on "The Monotheistic Tradition.")

The martyrdom of James at the hands of the Romans in 64 A.D., and the final destruction of Jerusalem by Titus six years later, dispersed this "hard line" group of Jewish Christians but by no means terminated their influence among the communities of the Diaspora.

If all this is so, what possible set of circumstances could have resulted in setting a shipload of Jewish Christians adrift on the Ocean Sea bound for an unknown destination at the feckless will of wind and current? The plainest clue to the answer to this question is that found in the legend of Itzamna as reported by the Spanish friar, Diego de Landa:

> Some of the old people of Yucatan say that they have heard from their ancestors that this land was occupied by a race of people who came from the east and who God delivered by opening twelve paths through the sea. If this were true it necessarily follows that all the inhabitants of the Indies are descendants of the Jews, since having once passed the Straits of Magellan they must have extended over more than two thousand leagues of land which now Spain governs.

One cannot follow de Landa's tortuous reasoning or agree with his conclusion that the American Indians were Jews, but the passage is significant in its mention of the *deliverance* of the strangers. The statement by Antonio de Herrera, quoted at the head of this chapter, is even more explicit: "God had *freed* them from other peoples by opening a road for them through the sea."

A highly significant feature of de Landa's account is the reference to the "twelve paths." As has been mentioned earlier, the Mayan system of numeration was vigesimal. It would have been infinitely more natural for them to refer to ten or twenty paths. I can find no reference to any Mayan calculations in dozens. On the other hand, twelve was for the Jews a sacred number – the number of the tribes of Israel, and of the Apostles of Jesus.

147

Chapter Seventeen

THE OLD WORLD REFUGEE

. . . I have taken this course with those who were accused before me as Christians: I have asked them whether they were Christians. Those who confessed I asked a second and a third time, threatening punishment. Those who persisted I ordered led away to execution.

— Pliny the Younger to the Emperor Trajan.

If the various assumptions made up to this point are correct, then we must look for the original overseas home of Quetzalcoatl somewhere in the Near East among a Semitic people, members of a Christian group, bearded, customarily wearing long, flowing robes and affecting a kind of Phrygian cap, who were forced to leave their homes through some kind of external pressure in the period between 100 and 150 A.D.

The early Christians were persecuted by the Romans almost from the beginning, partly because of their refusal to acknowledge the state cult of the emperor but also because they drew their membership from oppressed minorities. Their position has been compared not without reason to that of the Communist Party and other dissident groups in the United States in the twentieth century.

Before looking for a group of Christians desperate enough to attempt escape on the open waters of the Atlantic, it will be necessary to review in brief the events in the history of Christianity from the crucifixion of Christ about 33 A.D. to the opening years of the second Christian century.

What must first be realized is that for the first twenty years all Christians were Jews. Jesus was a Jew. The Apostles were Jews. What doctrine they followed was Jewish, deeply rooted in Jewish monotheism. Converts of the sect became Jews by the central rite of circumcision. The major difference between the Galileans (they were not yet called Christians) and the more orthodox branches of Jewry was their belief that the long-awaited Messiah had come in the person of Jesus of Nazareth, who had been adopted by God as His Son on the occasion of his baptism by John the Baptist.

Seven years after the Crucifixion the new sect met its first setback. The original apostles had chosen a man named Stephen as one of seven deacons appointed to a work of charity among the poor. Stephen was a Hellenist – that is, a circumcised Jew, probably from one of the communities of the Diaspora, whose native language was Greek. Stephen was a mystic and ecstatic who spoke out boldly against the sacrificial cult of the Temple. He was stoned to death by a mob led by one Saul of Tarsus.

Three years later this same Saul was converted on the road to Damascus by a blinding apprehension of the risen Jesus. The former persecutor and informer became himself a disciple of the Galilean. With frenetic energy he almost single-handedly created a universal church out of a schismatic Jewish sect. His self-appointed mission was to convert the Gentiles. In so doing he ran head-on into the keepers of the Galilean ministry – the Apostles. The clash is reported in the Book of the Acts of the Apostles. In that version Saul, who later took the Gentile Roman name, Paul, is of course the hero, for the book was written by his amanuensis and physician, St. Luke. Nevertheless, enough of the true nature of the dispute leaks through the narrative for us to reconstruct it, at least in part.

Circumcision was the principal issue but by no means the only one. Paul (to give him his Christian name) had grown up in a Greek city and had absorbed a great deal of Greek philosophy and Greek mysticism which showed up in his personal interpretation of the life, death, and resurrection of the Galilean. He was accused of heresy.

His main opposition came from Simon Peter and James, the brother of Jesus. It would seem that Peter later compromised his convictions with the views of the Tarsiote and met death with him in Rome in 64 A.D. James never altered his original conviction.

The Book of Acts would have us believe that the Council of Jerusalem ended on a reasonably amicable note with a victory for Paul. It is true that Paul won the war, but not that particular battle.

From this point on the Jewish and Gentile Christian churches went their separate ways, not without considerable conflict. The history of the Gentile churches is well known, being in essence the history of

Western Christianity. The history of the Jewish church is still being laboriously pieced together from the fragmentary remains of its literature.

The undisputed leader of the Jewish Christian church and its first bishop was James the Just, a brother of Jesus. A century after his death, a Jewish Christian, Hegesippus, wrote of James:

> He drank neither wine nor strong drink and he ate no meat. No razor touched his head and he did not anoint himself with oil, nor did he go to the baths. He alone was permitted to enter the sanctuary, for he did not wear wool but linen. Alone he used to enter the Temple, where he would be found kneeling and beseeching forgiveness for the people, and his knees grew calloused like those of a camel, because of his endless worship of God.[1]

James preached a stern and uncompromising ethic based on Jesus' teachings on material values:

> Let the brother of low degree rejoice in that he is exalted:
> But the rich, in that he is made low: because as the flower of the grass he shall pass away.
> For the sun is no sooner risen with a burning heat, but it withereth the grass, and the flower thereof falleth, and the grace of the fashion of it perisheth; so also shall the rich man fade away in his ways.[2]

Because of this determined insistence on the superior virtues of poverty, the sect gradually became known as the Ebionites (*ebionim* – the poor ones). The term was at first applied in a complimentary fashion but later, when the group was labelled heretical by the Gentile church, the expression was used contemptuously to imply poverty of *faith* and a presumptive leader called Ebion was invented to account for their descent into heresy.

Even a cursory study of the Gospels indicates that the Ebionite approach to material values was authentically that of Jesus of Nazareth. Later hands altered the Gospel teaching to remove or soften this uncompromising element. The beatitudes were touched up where there was a possibility of offending the establishment. "Blessed be ye poor"[3] became "blessed are the poor in spirit,"[4] a subtle mutilation of the original intent by which the Gospel was made more palatable to the middle and upper classes, especially among the Gentiles.

James worshipped at the Temple, Hegesippus says. However, from the beginning the apostolic group opposed the Temple's sacrificial cult. This became finally the excuse for semi-formal action on the part of orthodox Jewry. About the year 62 A.D., at the time of the Passover, James was taken to the top step of the Temple where he was, in effect, called upon to recant his belief in Jesus as the Messiah. Hegesippus tells the story of what happened:

> The Scribes then, and the Pharisees set James on the pinnacle of the Temple and they cried out to him, saying, "Oh, Just One, to whom we should all give heed, tell us what the gate of Jesus is, for the people are straying after Jesus who was crucified." And in ringing tones he replied, "Why do you ask me about the Son of Man? He dwells in heaven at the right hand of the mighty power, and He will come on the clouds of heaven." Many were convinced by him and hailed the testimony of James, saying, "Hosanna to the Son of David."
>
> Then the Scribes and Pharisees spoke again, this time to one another. "We have blundered in providing such testimony to Jesus. Let us climb to the top and throw him down, so that they may be frightened and not believe in Him." . . . They went therefore to the top and threw down the Just. "Let us stone James, the Just," they said to each other, and because he had not been killed by the fall they stoned him. But twisting onto his knees he said, "Lord God, Father, forgive them, for they do not know what they are doing." As they hurled stones at him thus, one of the priests of the sons of Rechab, the son of Rechabim, to whom the prophet Jeremiah bore witness, cried out, "Stop! What are you doing? The Just is praying for you." One of the crowd, a fuller, took hold of a club, with which he used to beat out the clothes, and he struck the Just on the head, and in this way was he martyred. They buried him on the spot near the Temple, and his gravestone is still beside the Temple.[5]

Deprived of their leader and denied access to the Temple, the apostolic group fled first to Jericho and then across the Jordan river to Pella, a pagan city south and east of Nazareth and Capernaum, the site of the opening months of the public ministry of Jesus. Their new leader and second bishop was Simon bar Clopas, a cousin of Jesus of Nazareth (his mother was Mary, sister of Joseph the carpenter).

Meanwhile, the self-appointed apostle, Paul, with little or no real contact with the church of Jerusalem, was establishing Gentile churches in Ephesus, Galatia, Thessaly, Corinth, and elsewhere. There is no "Gospel According to St. Paul." He made it up as he went along and his Epistles have become the foundation of the church which was first nicknamed "Christian" about the year 51 A.D. [6]

While these theological events were being shaped, the political condition of the Jewish people was going from bad to worse. A series of grotesquely incompetent Roman governors and puppet kings had ruled Palestine for a century, and every single one of them had grossly mistaken the Jewish character and the nature of the Jewish faith. It remained for a politically appointed clown named Florus finally to ignite the powder keg. In a spirit of innocent merriment he seized the vestments of the high priest of the Temple and violated them with appropriate obscenities, during the feast of the Passover. The sacrilege inflamed all Jewry – Pharisees, Sadducees, Essenes, and Ebionites. All joined ranks with the Zealots – the political activist wing of Jewish nationalism. In May 66 A.D., open rebellion broke out throughout Palestine.

Four years later it was all over but not until the emperor Titus had committed an army of 80,000 to the reduction of Jerusalem. (By way of contrast, Alexander the Great carved out his empire with 32,000 men; Julius Caesar conquered Gaul and invaded Britain with a maximum strength of 25,000 men.) When the victorious Romans finally marched into the Holy City their vengeance was terrible. The Temple was levelled to the ground and its defenders were massacred. Tacitus, the Roman historian, estimates that 600,000 Jewish civilians were slaughtered in the aftermath of the siege.

That should have been the end of the matter. Rome had steamrollered other opponents into oblivion. Its great rival, Carthage, had been wiped from the earth and its ruins sown with salt. Israel, however, refused to stay dead. Scarcely had mourning ended for the Jerusalem dead when new rebellions against Roman power were being stewed in secret places.

The Romans never understood the Jews and were baffled by their religious sects, all of which were actively and belligerently monotheistic. Persecution of the Gentile Christians began in earnest under Nero (54-68 A.D.) and continued with varying degrees of severity until the reign of Constantine the Great (307-337 A.D.).

The Jewish Christians were particular objects of suspicion to the

Romans since they were physical descendants of those apostles who had followed the crucified "King of the Jews." In the reign of Domitian (81-96 A.D.), two grandsons of Jude (another brother of Jesus of Nazareth) by name Jacob and Zechariah were brought before the emperor on the accusation that they belonged to the line of David. They admitted the charge but, on questioning, said they were only poor farmers and that the kingdom of the Messiah Jesus was not of this world but was heavenly and angelic "and that it would become manifest when time had reached its consummation." Their diplomatic answers appeased the doubts of the emperor, and he released them and allowed them and their sect to live in peace. Of the later days of Jacob and Zechariah, Eusebius, the historian of the early church, reports:

> After their release they were numbered among the leaders of the churches, inasmuch as they had borne witness to their faith and because they belonged to the family of the Lord. With peace reestablished, they lived on until the era of Trajan.[7]

Orthodox Jewry was not so tolerant of the descendants of the apostles, nor was the Roman emperor, Trajan. In 90 A.D., the Jewish Christians were denied further participation in the worship of the synagogues, along with the Gentile Christians. In 107 A.D. Simon bar Clopas, second bishop of the Ebionites, was crucified by order of Trajan's governor, Atticus, on the familiar charge that he was a descendant of King David. Justin, who is believed also to have been a member of the family of the Messiah, became the third bishop of the sect.

The Ebionites were now in a position of very great peril. They had been proclaimed to be the enemies of both church and state. Their Jewish contemporaries had barred them from the Temple and the synagogues. The Gentile Christians had accused them of heresy. The jittery Romans, fearful of resurgent Jewish nationalism, sought their lives because they followed the heirs of the great Israelitic king, David. They drew farther and farther back, into the hinterlands of empire and into the anonymity of the larger cities. There were groups of them in Rome, in Alexandria, and on Cyprus, but the main body of the sect continued to pursue their independent faith in the lands east of the Jordan.

Meanwhile, Roman distrust centred on the growing Gentile Christian church, and there were more or less constant efforts to suppress it. One of the earliest surviving pagan references to Christianity has to do with an attempt to stamp out the cult in the province of Bithynia bordering the Euxine (Black) Sea. About 111 A.D., the emperor Trajan (98-117 A.D.) appointed Pliny the Younger to be legate and governor of Bithynia. Pliny was not quite sure how to handle the matter of the Christians. He did not know "what crime is usually punished or investigated or to what extent." He wrote to the emperor requesting instruction, at the same time transmitting to posterity a brief, tantalizing glimpse of the sect's ritual practices:

> They had been accustomed to assemble on a fixed day before daylight and sing by turns a hymn to Christ as a god; they bound themselves with an oath, not for any crime, but to commit neither theft, nor robbery, nor adultery, not to break their word and not to deny a deposit when demanded; after these things were done, it was their custom to depart and meet together again to take food, but ordinary and harmless food.

In his reply Trajan instructed his legate that Christians were not to be sought out nor tried on anonymous accusations but, if publicly accused and convicted, they were to be punished by death unless they were prepared to curse Christ and to "worship our gods," in which case a full pardon would be granted.

Pliny's service to the empire terminated with his death in 113 A.D., the very year in which the long-simmering Jewish pot boiled over again.

The opportunity was provided by an invasion of Roman territory by the Parthians. Trajan immediately marched against them and Jewry erupted. A major revolt broke out among the Jews in Palestine, Egypt, Antioch, Cyrene, and Cyprus. The fighting was savage and tens of thousands of Jews, Gentiles, and Jewish Christians were killed in battle, murdered, or executed. The Jewish Christians, being by far the smallest of the three groups and the most feared, sustained the greatest losses. The remnants continued to appoint bishops to govern them until about 135 A.D. The last of the episcopal line of whom we have record was Judas Kyriakos. His surname indicates quite strongly that he too was descended from the family of Jesus of Nazareth (*kurios* – Lord).

The third, and last, great Jewish revolt against Roman rule was that led by Simon bar Kokhba from 132 to 135 A.D. Following the collapse of that rebellion the history of the Ebionites, for all practical purposes, ends. Their influence can be traced through subsequent "heretical" movements within Christianity and, according to Hans-Joachim Schoeps,[8] within the faith of Islam.

Gentile Christianity, of course, survived partly because it was able to rationalize the promised return of the Christ, which the apostles expected within their lifetimes,[9] to some indefinite future and also because the new church, following Paul's example, absorbed or compromised with those articles of pagan belief which it could not successfully counter. Thus the Gentile cult became mystic, supernatural, sacrificial, sacramental, liturgical, and soteriological. That is to say, Jesus' birth was made magical and his death on the cross was made to be a blood sacrifice for the atonement of sin; it was made sacred by the pre-ordination of God, commemorated in rigidly ritualistic and liturgical terms and incorporated within the ancient sun myth of Osiris, the resurrected god of Egypt, whose sky symbol was Sothis (Sirius) the yearly rising of which on the horizon was the sign for the rebirth of the earth.

Some of the theological differences between the Ebionites and their Jewish and Christian enemies have already been mentioned. These and other differences must now carefully be noted.

The birth of Jesus was in no way supernatural. He was physically the son of Joseph and hence a direct descendant of David and heir to the prophets. He was not and could not have been "co-eternal with God" since God must have existed first in order to "beget" a son.

Jesus was the True Prophet, the second Moses, the Messianic Son of Man. He was adopted by God as His son when he was baptized by John the Baptist, at which time the Spirit of God descended on him in the form of a dove.

He came not to destroy the Law, but to reform it. He rejected blood sacrifice as repugnant to God and he believed in the superior virtues of poverty.

Jesus taught the resurrection of the body and he himself rose from death. He had come into the world in humility but would return in glory.

He taught that baptism by water is necessary for the forgiveness of sins and for entrance into the kingdom of heaven.

In accord with this interpretation of the person of Jesus, the Ebionites rejected vigourously the Gentile Christian view of the death of Jesus on the cross as a vicarious atoning sacrifice for sins. Atonement was obtained through water baptism and the confession of sin. Since Jesus followed the Law, admission to the new faith must be made under the Law, that is, by circumcision. The Lord's Supper was maintained as a meal of fellowship, a memorial to the Messiah, with no ritualistic paraphernalia. They idealized the state of poverty, prohibited the eating of meat, were opposed to secular monarchic institutions, believed in the imminence of the second coming and admitted the existence of angels and demons, to the extent that some of the sect believed that an archangel entered the physical body of Jesus at the time of his baptism and adoption by God.

Of particular importance to this study are certain features of Ebionite belief and practice.

In the first place, they practised a rigid form of monotheism. The worship of God the Creator and primal force is persistent and unvarying. This is also certainly the central theme in the worship inaugurated in the Americas by Quetzalcoatl and his comrades.

A belief in the resurrection of the body is perhaps second in point of importance in the faith of the Jewish Christians. This, too, is demonstrated throughout the area influenced by the great religious revival of the second century in the Americas.

The cleansing of sin by baptism in water was central in the belief of the Ebionites. Water, by itself, became a symbol of cleanliness and purity. Members of the Jewish sect were fanatics in the matter of personal cleanliness, bathing or washing before meals, before prayer, before any secular or spiritual act. At the same time ritual baptism for the remission of sins was a once-only act in the believer's lifetime and was approached with great solemnity. It is hardly necessary to refer to the overwhelming importance of water in the pre-Columbian American religious beliefs, or to the sanctity of the formal rite of baptism. Daily lustrations are still a feature of Mayan life today.

Second only to the importance of the water element in the Ebionite faith was that of the movement of the air. The spirit of God was that wind upon the water that signalled the act of creation. Here again it is hardly necessary to mention the pre-eminent position of the wind-gods in the ancient American religions.

Of somewhat lesser importance are the nature of the Eucharistic meal, which both among the Ebionites and among the civilizations of the Americas was a sacramental and memorial meal, but not a liturgical act; the belief in the return of the Messiah which finds its echo among the Americans in the legend of the promised *parousia* of Quetzalcoatl, and the Ebionite belief in the existence of angels and demons, with which pre-Columbian American art and religion are plentifully endowed.

In sum, what we know of the beliefs and practices initiated in the Americas by the alien teacher, Quetzalcoatl, is compatible with the theory that Quetzalcoatl and his comrades were Jewish Christians – Ebionites.

In our search for the origin of the Quetzalcoatl expedition we must turn our attention to the island of Cyprus. There was an Ebionite colony there for which we have biblical verification. In that confusing and much-tampered-with Book of the Acts of the Apostles we are told:

> Meanwhile those who had been scattered after the persecution that arose over Stephen made their way to Phoenicia, Cyprus and Antioch, bringing the message to Jews only and to no others.[10]

Barnabas, a Levite, who although he was not one of The Twelve was styled an apostle, was a native of Cyprus and evangelized there. There had long been Jews on Cyprus. In the eighth century B.C., while the Assyrian power was ravaging the little kingdoms of Palestine many fled there from Tyre and Sidon for refuge:

> You shall busy yourselves no more, you, the sorely oppressed virgin city of Sidon. Though you arise and cross over to Kittim, even there you shall find no rest.[11]

Cyprus was known in the Old Testament Hebrew as Kittim or Chittim. It has been noted previously that in the surviving passages of the book of Votan, culture-hero of the Tzendals, we are told that the hero returned four times to his ancestral home, the land of Chivim. The correspondence in the names is close.

PART VI

CONCLUSIONS

Chapter Eighteen

THE MAN OF IZAMAL

Quetzalcoatl was the culture-hero of Tula. Before he became divine, he was a man. He was priest, ruler, demiurge, then God; he lorded it over Tula for twenty-two years, lost a civil war, and was forced into exile. . . . The time given to this historical fact is A.D. 116.

– Victor W. von Hagen, *World of the Maya.*

1

We started out on this quest for the historical Quetzalcoatl with the legend that details his deeds. We found that geographically and chronologically this legend belongs in the roster of the world's great myths, along with the stories of Gilgamesh, the Trojan Wars, and King Arthur of Camelot. Myth has been found again and again to conceal true history. Gilgamesh was, in the beginning, someone. The Trojan Wars did take place. King Arthur did live. So did Jesus of Nazareth. So did Quetzalcoatl.

The epic of Gilgamesh profoundly influenced the Hebrew interpretation of history. The Trojan Wars, as recounted by Homer, influenced the course of European literature. King Arthur's romantic story deeply affected the culture of Europe. Quetzalcoatl of Teotihuacán and Jesus of Nazareth effected a religious revolution which still affects the lives of half the world's people.

Sifting through the orally transmitted evidence of the story of Quetzalcoatl, we find certain features that are consistent in all the many retellings of the legend:

1. He was white and bearded.
2. He came from the east, from across the ocean.
3. He was a fugitive from his own land.
4. He came a very long time ago.

161

5. He taught a gentle faith and was opposed to human or animal sacrifice.

Whoever he was and whatever he taught, he and his faith were acceptable to the peoples to whom he came. He and his followers posed no threat to them.[1] They offered simply a new way of looking at the relationship between God and man; between the Creator and his Creation. To the introspective Americans this was both challenging and exciting. The bearer of the new philosophy was revered during his lifetime and deified after his departure or death.

The enormous influence exerted by this spiritual approach to life and living was still discernible 1,500 years later. It gave rise to new and enduring forms of native art and literature. It is no exaggeration to say that the influence of Quetzalcoatl on American art, culture, literature, and religion can be compared only to that of Gautama Buddha in Asia, Mohammed in the Near East, and Jesus of Nazareth in Europe.

Following the initial revelation, all religions depend for popular support on ritual and liturgical practices which crystallize and mythologize the essential elements of faith. In Christianity the essential elements are: purification of the body (baptism), purification of the soul (confession and absolution), propitiation of the deity (prayer), sacrifices by proxy (the Lord's Supper), the identification of the worshipper with God by his own sacrifice (the offering of goods or services), and the reward – life after death (the Resurrection). All of these liturgical practices were found by the sixteenth-century Spanish friars in the New World. All were associated with the name of the American culture-hero Quetzalcoatl or his successors in the high priesthood.

2

The legend of Quetzalcoatl does not stand unsupported. Factual, that is to say, archaeological, evidence strongly reinforces the impression that an alien element was interjected into the high cultures of the Americas at a period remote from the present. The evidence ranges from the general to the specific. Generally speaking there is a mass of artifactual material to be found all the way from the Mississippi basin to the *altiplano* of Peru and Bolivia that indicates that an event of far-reaching consequences, of a religious nature, occurred some time in the opening centuries of the Christian era. In what is generally accepted as the nuclear area of this intrusive cultural and religious element – the shores of the Gulf of Mexico and the land areas contiguous to it – hundreds of artifacts have been found which do not fit in with what we know of the pre-historic autochthonous cultures.

Chief among these artifacts are figures in terracotta and other materials which in no way resemble classic American Indian types. On the contrary they convey strong impressions of being portraits of persons whose origin was in Europe. The racial characteristics most commonly portrayed are those which we associate with the Semitics of the Eastern Mediterranean. Of outstanding importance is a group of portrait images found in several states of Mexico, in Guatemala, Peru, and Bolivia which can be construed as representing the same individual at different stages in his life. I have identified this individual as the prototypal Quetzalcoatl.

In the same nuclear area where the legend of Quetzalcoatl was apparently spawned there have been found two bearded images which have been identified as of European manufacture and datable to the second century of the Christian era.

Hundreds of miles to the north, in the states of Kentucky and Tennessee, Roman and Jewish coins of the second century have been discovered in addition to a Hebrew inscription recording a date during the Second Jewish Rebellion (132-135 A.D.)

Scattered throughout Central and South America carvings and rock art have been found using Greek, Roman, and Phoenician characters as well as some symbols identical with syllabic characters used on the island of Cyprus from very ancient times.

In addition powerful physiological evidence has been presented by Thor Heyerdahl in his magnum opus, *American Indians in the Pacific*. Many of the "mummy bundles" found by the thousands in the dry coastal plains of South America contain the skeletal or mummified remains of persons who in life were above the average stature of the Indian natives of the area and had blonde, brownish or red wavy hair. The type of hair, bone and skull structure are European or Caucasoid in character.

Numerically, in short, the instances of an apparent inter-reaction between European and American cultures at an early date warrant serious consideration. There are quite literally hundreds of them.

So impressive is this constellation of materials that it is actually more difficult to refute them, item by item, jot and tittle, root and branch, than it is to accept them. Yet an enormous amount of energy has been dissipated doing just that. Thor Heyerdahl cites an extreme example of this wasteful practice. A scholarly writer marshalled an array of sixty remarkable parallels between two restricted areas within the Old and New Worlds. In his description of this assembly he called it "a substantial list of specific cultural features of limited distribution which were shared by cultures of the ancient Andean area and the ancient Mediterranean prior to the Middle Ages."[2] The purpose of his work was not to prove that a contact existed but quite the opposite. He used the list as "proof" that the most impressive array of parallelisms can arise independently through evolutionary processes. Why did he not come to the infinitely simpler conclusion that these features were transmitted from one place to another? Because, he said, the two areas – the Andes and the Mediterranean – were too far apart! This kind of circular thinking has marred much of the academic work on the prehistory of the Americas and has in its own way effected as much harm to the search for truth as the equally circular thinking of such fanatics as Ignatius Donnelly.

3

From a consideration of this mass of evidence I offer the following conclusions:

The man known among the Mexicans as Quetzalcoatl was an historical personage who landed with his followers on the coast of the Gulf of Mexico after completing a transatlantic voyage from Europe some time in the first half of the second Christian century, most probably in the first quarter of that century.

He and many of his companions were Jews and, in consequence, monotheists. They were not, however, "Temple Jews" since Quetzalcoatl reportedly rejected blood sacrifice, an unvarying feature of the worship of the Temple at Jerusalem from its foundation.

From this and a collection of liturgical practices associated with the cult of Quetzalcoatl a close correspondence may be established between the faith taught by Quetzalcoatl and that followed by the schismatic Jewish sect known as the Ebionites.

At the beginning of the second century there were Ebionite colonies in Pella, beyond the Jordan, in the great city of Alexandria and on the island of Cyprus. It was from one of these colonies that Quetzalcoatl and his comrades must have come, fleeing from the wrath of their enemies:

> God had freed them from other peoples by opening a road for them through the sea.

The inland position of Pella makes it unlikely that they came from there. Alexandria was a Roman city where the shipping was more likely to be closely guarded. Cyprus (Hebrew Chittim) is the most likely source of the Quetzalcoatl expedition. The island was familiar ground to both Jewish and Gentile Christians. There was a large Jewish population there and many synagogues.[3] Also we have the tantalizing reference in the story of Votan to "Chivim" as being the homeland of the hero. The port of Paphos on the Mediterranean would have been a logical site for the assembling of the refugees.

There was no lack of Jewish refugees on Cyprus in the last two years of Trajan's reign. The Jewish uprising there was particularly savage. One ancient writer reports that the rebels slaughtered 240,000 Greeks and Romans before the revolt was crushed. The Roman Senate acted swiftly and with great severity. It was decreed that all Jews be banished from the island, never again to set foot on Cyprus under pain of death. There is some reason to believe that the rebels, led by one Artemion, claimed as their victims not only Greeks and Romans but Christians as well – both Jewish and Gentile Christians.

Here then, between 115 and 117 A.D., we have a great mass of thousands of Jews seeking escape by sea from ancient Chittim. Most of the refugees probably sheltered in the communities of the Diaspora within the great cities of the Empire – Alexandria, Antioch, Tarsus in Cilicia, even in Rome itself. But where could the survivors of the Ebionite colony on Cyprus go? Wherever they went on the shores of the Mediterranean they faced persecution by the Romans, the Jews, and the Gentile Christians. The only sea-lanes open to them were to the westward . . . past the Pillars of Hercules . . . somewhere on the shores of the Ocean Sea.

> God had freed them from other peoples by opening a road for them through the sea.

Sometime in the year 116 A.D. a vessel weighed anchor in the port of Paphos. Behind them the clear skies of Cyprus were sullied by the smoke and flames of anarchy and pillage. Silently the ship slipped out into the waters of the Mediterranean and turned its prow westward.

I doubt very much if the crew and passengers knew where they were going. Flight from immediate danger must have been their first consideration. The second was escape from the sphere of Roman influence. They could have provisioned their ship at any one of dozens of Mediterranean ports. Then on they went, perhaps by night, through the Pillars of Hercules.

Where to next? Not to Britain or Gaul, for the Roman writ ran there, too. Perhaps to the west coast of Africa or the Canary Islands, which had been long known to the Phoenicians, Greeks, and Romans. Perhaps they were consciously bound farther still to the half-legendary Isles of the Blessed, far to the west over the Ocean Sea.

Who was their pilot? Perhaps a seasoned seaman from Tyre or Sidon, or a Jew from Jappa, heir to a thousand years of navigational knowledge of the waters from Iceland to the Cape of Good Hope, from Britain to no man knew how far west.

Once on the open Atlantic the course of their voyage probably depended to a large extent on the vagaries of wind and current. They could, under certain conditions, tack into the wind (despite modern misconceptions about ancient navigation) but they had no compass and no precise navigational aids. They could estimate with reasonable degree of accuracy the latitude of their position but had no means of establishing longitude.

It can be speculated that somewhere off the Canaries they were captured by the Canary Current and borne south and west. With the unseen coast of Africa on their left they may have entered the slower-moving North Equatorial Stream and so been carried south of Hispaniola and Jamaica through the Yucatan Channel and into the Gulf of Mexico where the clockwise Gulf current would deposit them eventually on the Mexican shoreline, probably not far from Veracruz.

It is easily said, but it must have been a long, arduous, and uncertain voyage. There would have been deaths from disease and misadventure. Their stock of provisions must have given out long before the journey ended. The fishes of the sea would have provided a sufficient if monotonous diet. Water would have posed a more difficult problem but that could have been solved by the use of rain water and the dew from the sails, rigidly rationed.

There is no question to believe that their reception was anything but friendly. Nearly 1,400 years later Christopher Columbus and his men were welcomed with kindness on the islands of the West Indies. The aboriginal inhabitants of the Americas seem nearly always to have been generous and hospitable in their treatment of the European strangers. It has only been when their trust has been betrayed, their women raped, and their lands taken from them that the native Americans have risen against the Europeans.

Unlike those who came a millennium and more later, the transatlantic voyagers of the second century had no interest in material riches. The Ebionite vow of poverty would have saved them from those temptations. They were interested only in the souls of men. They were burning to tell their American hosts of the one True God, of his care for men, of the coming of the new age. They were working against time for they believed that the *parousia* – the second coming of the Messiah – was near at hand.

There is overwhelming evidence that the new faith was well received. Within a century it had spread to every corner of the New World where civilized people lived. It did not totally oust the old faith in the gods of America but it did alter and soften the ancient beliefs. Gentile Christianity was no more successful in obliterating either the knowledge or the worship of the old gods of Roman, Greek, and Scandinavian mythology. The English names of the very days of our week attest the longevity of the "old ones." [4]

The policy of the newcomers in seeking places for the worship of God followed an age-old practice. Ancient shrines of the old gods were preserved and put to the use of the new faith. The instructions of Pope Gregory to St. Augustine in the sixth century A.D. give us a good example of this usage in Gentile Christianity:

> I have come to the conclusion that the temples of the idols in England should not on any account be destroyed. Augustine must smash the idols, but the temples themselves should be sprinkled with holy water and altars set up in them in which relics are to be enclosed. For we ought to take advantage of well-built temples by

purifying them from devil-worship and dedicating them to the service of the true God. In this way, I hope the people (seeing their temples are not destroyed) will leave their idolatry and yet continue to frequent the places as formerly, so coming to know and revere the true God.[5]

How long Quetzalcoatl remained among the peoples of the Gulf Coast is impossible to say, but by 125 A.D. at the latest he was rebuilding the great city of Teotihuacán and, shortly thereafter or perhaps at the same time, the great works at Cholula were under way. Victor W. von Hagen was, of course, in error in the excerpt from one of his popular works cited at the head of this chapter, when he attributed the date of 116 A.D. to the city of Tula. That city was a much later foundation and the priest of Quetzalcoatl who bore the hero's name was the eleventh-century Prince Topiltzin.

The legendary references to the length of Quetzalcoatl's stay among various peoples are not to be taken literally. The span of twenty years so often used in this connection merely meant a considerable time, as in the many references in the Christian Bible to forty days or forty years. The numbers in both cases have a sacred, symbolical significance.

I believe that Quetzalcoatl, the leader himself, travelled extensively on missionary journeys throughout the New World.[6] I do not believe, however, that he visited personally all the places where his cult later became established.

I believe that he was the Mayan Itzamna but not the Tzendals' Votan, who was of a later generation. He may have visited the Quiché-Maya of Guatemala, although the existing record of the *Popul Vuh* seems to me merely a somewhat garbled version of the Yucatecan story. I believe that he was the gentle and aged Bochica of the Mochica but not the Viracocha or Thunupa of Tiahuanaco. The bearded images of the Tiahuanaco civilization are such as would have been made by those who had not seen the original, but merely heard of his appearance.

From his extensive travels in Central and South America Quetzalcoatl returned to Yucatan, to the shrine of Izamal. There, revered almost already as a god, old, bent, with but a single tooth in his head, he died some time before the end of the second century A.D.

Of all the places where his legend lingered, only in Yucatan is the story brought to this conclusion. Elsewhere the legend promises a return of the hero. In Yucatan, at Izamal, the brooding pyramids mark the sorrow of his adopted people at the passing of the great priest, Itzamna of the healing hands, the unknown Apostle of the Americas.

We have forged in this book a long, long chain of events. Some of the links may be weak. I believe that most of them will withstand testing.

Let me now add a final link in the chain.

If the second-century establishment in Mexico was European, then it was Christian or, at the very least, influenced by Christian elements.

If it was Christian, then for all the various reasons I have outlined it was Jewish Christian.

If it was Jewish Christian, then its founders were members of the sect known as the Ebionites.

If it was Ebionitic, the founders were heirs of the original apostolic group.

If it was apostolic, its membership would have come from some of the physical descendants of the first followers of Jesus.

Since the leadership of the apostolic group for the first century after the crucifixion of Jesus came invariably from his own family, it is entirely possible that Quetzalcoatl was a relative of Jesus of Nazareth.

In that case, Izamal is one of the world's great holy cities.

It has been a long journey
God be with you.

PART VII

OTHER
TRAVELLERS

Chapter Nineteen

STRANGERS IN A STRANGE LAND

Professor Ralph Linton, late distinguished anthropologist of Yale, in a book review published in *American Antiquity*, the official journal of American archaeology, said of Harold S. Gladwin, who had written a book suggesting, among other things, that survivors of Alexander the Great's wrecked fleet found their way to America in the fourth century B.C. and were responsible for some of the great prehistoric civilizations of this hemisphere: "Mr. Gladwin approaches the problem of American origins with the tentative jocularity of an elderly gentleman patting a new secretary's posterior. If she objects, he can lament her lack of a sense of humour; if she does not, the next moves are obvious."

– Robert Wauchope, *Lost Tribes and Sunken Continents*.

1

In this amusing and somewhat acerbic little book from which I have quoted above, Dr. Robert Wauchope has dealt severely with the great number of theories that have been advanced to account for the flowering of civilization on the American continents. I have now added myself to the number of those unfortunates destined to know the sting of Dr. Wauchope's rope of nettles. I must however point out a distinction that may gain for me a lighter sentence – in no place in this book do I attribute the founding of the ancient American civilizations to the descendants of James and Jude.

As I indicated in the Foreword, I have merely, like Mr. Gladwin, opened up the subject. The next move is up to my readers – including Dr. Wauchope (whom God preserve) of New Orleans.

2

My express purpose in this book has been to examine the legend of Quetzalcoatl as it relates to certain events of the opening centuries of the Christian era. I do not intend by this to deny the possibility of other contacts, transatlantic or transPacific, between the Old World and the New.

Gordon Ekholm and Robert Heine-Geldern have made a strong case for the importation of some culture elements into Middle America from Southeast Asia as has been briefly noted on page 84. This possible contact has been set at a date between 100 and 600 A.D.

The strange case of the Jomon pottery is much earlier and much more fascinating. A midden site at Valdivia, on the coast of Ecuador, discovered by an amateur archaeologist, Emilio Estrada, yielded pottery which under Carbon 14 analysis revealed a surprising age – 4,450 years before the present time. This was half a millenium older than the earliest American pottery previously known. Unlike the later examples of American ceramic art, it showed no initial development. It was just suddenly there, the work of people with an already well-advanced technical knowledge in this field. Two members of the Smithsonian Institution at Washington became interested in the finds. After closely examining 36,096 pieces of pottery from Valdivia they could find only one parallel for the designs employed there – and that parallel came from the oldest Asiatic ceramic tradition, a type called Jomon from its typical Japanese site, 8,000 sailing miles away from Ecuador.

The controversy that raged following the announcement of this extraordinary theory – that a boatload of prehistoric Japanese fishermen had crossed the vast Pacific 2,000 years before the birth of Christ – created considerably more heat than illumination. The identification of the pottery has been challenged again and again, but largely, it is interesting to note, in only the most general terms. Since the parallel was noted by accredited archaeologists, working under carefully controlled conditions and after examining a large number of specimens, the criticism has been discreetly muted. Dr. Wauchope does not attack the theory directly, contenting himself rather by describing the Valdivia supposition in a chapter dealing with such far-out fictions as the descent of the Americans from the lost continent of Atlantis or the Pacific continent of Mu, thus subtly condemning the Jomon story by juxtaposition.

Although speculation of this type has always been angrily denounced by conservative Americanists, I can see no reason for rejecting out of hand the possibility of drift voyages such as the one that must have brought Japanese fishermen to Valdivia. Considering the length of time that mankind has been a water-borne creature, such unintentional voyages must have been successfully accomplished more than once in the past 6,000 years.

What must be made clear, however, is that there is no evidence whatever to indicate that the high cultures of the Americas sprang from such random contacts. The Jomon pottery influence, for example, affected only a small area and made no lasting impact on the development of the native culture even in that area.

Whatever technical skills Quetzalcoatl and his comrades brought from the eastern Mediterranean had little or no influence on the already well-established indigenous technology. What influence they did exert was in the field of religion and ritual and that influence, as I have tried to indicate, was enormous.

Random appearances of objects found out of context have often been reported and their meaning debated, sometimes with great ferocity. Rune stones in Minnesota, towers in Massachusetts, altars in New Hampshire, the image of a supposed mediaeval knight elsewhere in New England, "Carthaginian" inscriptions in South America – all have had their supporters and detractors.

In the great majority of these instances the reported objects have been found in splendid isolation with no matrix of supporting evidence. The proponents of a Viking penetration of the interior of North America have on the whole been more fortunate than the rest, or perhaps merely more assiduous. Their claims are based on a more solid foundation than those of almost any other group, for after all there is substantial proof that the Norsemen did in fact reach the shores of America. Their cause has been gravely injured, however, by some rather too-exuberant amateurs who have on occasion overstepped the bounds of scientific propriety – as in the case of the disputed Kensington rune stone.

Supposed resemblances of singular American artifacts to European or Asiatic prototypes have been summoned out of the past to support claims that the ancient Americans were really descendants of the Phoenicians, Assyrians, ancient Egyptians, Canaanites, Trojans, Romans, Etruscans, Greeks, Scythians, Tartars, Chinese Buddhists, Hindus, Africans, Irish, Welsh, Basques, Portuguese, French, Spaniards, and Huns.

Even more numerous have been the attempts to prove connections between the languages of the New World and those of the Old. That extraordinary fanatic, Ignatius Donnelly, sought in the last century to link the language of the Maya with the mysterious and unique tongue spoken by the Spanish Basques, attempting to trace them both to the language of the Cro-Magnon men who executed the magnificent cave murals of France and Spain 10,000 to 20,000 years ago.

Donnelly had many successors and imitators who have announced from time to time the discovery of Welsh and Irish words in the tribal tongues of North American Indians. A. Hyatt Verrill marshalled an impressive number of words of similar spelling, sound, and meaning in ancient Sumerian and the languages of South America. Thor Heyerdahl has claimed to trace affinities between the ancient Peruvian tongues and the languages spoken in the Pacific islands. Such linguistic exercises, while fascinating in themselves, have so far presented nothing like the quality or quantity of proof required to bolster such claims. It may be that when we know a great deal more than we do now about the history of human speech patterns we may be able to analyze the number of similarities that do in fact exist and trace them to their sources. At present, however, our knowledge in this field is far too inexact to serve as a means of discovering the geographical origins of peoples.

In all except two instances, the identification of alleged transoceanic voyagers rests on evidence that is far too flimsy to be widely acceptable. An aberrant artifact, a structure of unknown provenance, a puzzling monument are insufficient bases on which to build a substantial theory.

One of the two exceptions to this general rule is the individual or individuals with which this book has attempted to deal. The convergence of a mass of evidence, legendary and scientific, on a specific period and a specific kind of person of a clearly defined personal character, who introduced a new kind of thinking about the relationship between man and creation makes the story of Quetzalcoatl susceptible of intensive study and in the end, I believe, capable of such proof as to satisfy the most sceptical and conservative scholarship.

The second exception is that other figure – white, bearded, and alien – whose story runs through the Quetzalcoatl legend like an errant and confusing thread; the man who was known in Mexico as Prince Topiltzin, "Our Lord Ce Ácatl Quetzalcoatl." There is now no doubt about the historicity of Prince Topiltzin, that conquering apostle who, driven out of his own city, Tula, by a rebellious citizenry, took himself and his followers to Yucatan where deification was later granted to him and his successors as Kukulcan. Topiltzin-Kukulcan has approximate dates. He was very much later than Quetzalcoatl. His revived cult of the Feathered Serpent found little lasting favour with the Maya who remained true to the earlier revelation of Itzamna of the healing hands.

The distinction between the two legendary figures, who lived nearly a thousand years apart, is fuzzy and often contradictory in Mexico proper; in Yucatan the two men are clearly separated in legend and in the memories of the people. In Central and South America the threads are again interwoven to the point of confusion. Here and there the second Quetzalcoatl becomes a little clearer by virtue of a more recent memory and by a distinctive difference in personal character.

Naymlap, for instance, comes to the people of Lambayeque with a numerous retinue of concubines, officers, administrators, and tax-collectors to found a dynasty and to take over the rule of the people. He is a much different person from the dimly remembered old and gentle Bochica or Zume who came down from the north to teach the clever Mochica the things they should know about themselves and God.

If I read the archetypal legend of Quetzalcoatl correctly, it was his priest, Prince Topiltzin, who departed from his people "on a raft of serpents" somewhere on the Gulf Coast of Mexico. It was Prince Topiltzin who was remembered as wearing the *dark* flowing robe which is sometimes referred to in the legends as bearing crosses on its material.

The Kukulcan who is depicted on the doorpost of the pyramid-temple bearing his name at Chichén Itzá is European in type with a long, flowing beard, but he does not at all resemble the portrait images of the earlier Quetzalcoatl. His arrogant behaviour, his often harsh rule, his penchant for walled and fortified cities (Mayapán in Yucatan, for example) – all these suit well with the identification of this figure as that of a European voyager-adventurer of the High Middle Ages. Considering his approximate period – 950 to 1100 A.D. – his appearance, his cross-decorated robes, and his serpent-raft vessel he might well have been a Norse or Irish seafarer opportunistically founding a New World dynasty in the same fashion in which the Viking captain-warriors established royal houses in Normandy, Sicily, Russia, and England.

The extent of the Norse and Irish voyages on the Atlantic are as yet unknown. Records are scanty; the Icelandic sagas often conceal as much as they reveal, and the archaeological evidence is very thin indeed. Nevertheless the sailors who were capable of navigating the icy, fog-bound seas of the North Atlantic between Scotland and Iceland and Greenland, Greenland and Newfoundland would surely not have been daunted by the warmer seas of the South Atlantic with a following and favourable wind.

Of all the shadowy figures that inhabit the fringes of the great central American hero epic of Quetzalcoatl, Prince Topiltzin is the most corporeal and the most susceptible of critical and analytical examination.

But that is another story.

Notes

PART I — THE LEGEND

Chapter One — Quetzalcoatl

1. *The Song of Quetzalcoatl* , translated from the Aztec by John Hubert Cornyn (Yellow Springs, Ohio: Antioch Press, 2d ed., 1931). Quoted in Constance Irwin, *Fair Gods and Stone Faces* , pp. 35-6.
2. *The Art of Ancient Mexico* , Chapter 3, pp. 48-60.
3. Rene Millon, Bruce Drewitt and James A. Bennyhoff. *The Pyramid of the Sun at Teotihuacán: 1959 Investigations* (Philadelphia: The American Philosophical Society, 1965),p. 5.
4. *The Indian Art of Mexico and Central America* , pp. 136-7.

Chapter Two — Itzamna and Kukulcan

1. Gregory Mason, *Silver Cities of Yucatan* , Preface. It is obvious that Spinden confused Topiltzin, the original Kukulcan, with the later Toltec ruler, Huemac, and combined the achievements of both in one person.
2. Quoted in Laurette Sejourné, *Burning Water* , pp. 9-10. She also quotes Sahagún's caution to the incredulous: "What is written down in this volume, no human being would have sufficient understanding to invent, nor could any living man contradict the language that therein is, so that if all the Indians who understand these things were questioned, they would affirm that this is the language proper to their ancestors and the works they did."
3. *Historia Antigua de Yucatan* , p. 144.

Chapter Three — Votan

1. Quoted in Antonio del Rio, *Description of the Ruins of an Ancient City Discovered Near Palenque* (London: 1822) pp. 34-6.
2. *Fair Gods and Stone Faces.*
3. *Geschichte der amerikanischen Urreligionem* (Basel: 1855), pp. 486-90.
4. *Mexican and Central American Mythology* , p. 136.
5. *American Hero-Myths* , p. 218.

Chapter Five – Bochica and Naymlap

1. *American Hero-Myths* , p. 220.
2. *Historia General de las Conquistas del Nuevo Reyno de Granada* , Lib. I Cap. III.

Chapter Six – Viracocha and Thunupa

1. The birth of John the Baptist is commemorated on June 24; his death by behead-
ing on August 29.
2. Recorded by Cristobal de Molina: *Relacion de muchas cosas scaecidos en el Peru*
(1552). English translation from Edward Hyams and George Ordish, *The Last of
the Incas* , p. 95.

PART II – THE ARCHAEOLOGICAL EVIDENCE

Chapter Seven – The Great Awakening

1. *Pre-Inca Art and Culture* , p. 17.
2. *Ibid* , p. 180.
3. Melville Jacobs and Bernhard J. Stern, *General Anthropology* , p. 40.

Chapter Eight – The Bearded Faces

1. *Pre-Columbian Terracottas* , p. 11.
2. A peculiar survival of this ancient Mexican veneration for bearded persons is
instanced in Jacques Soustelle's *The Four Suns* , pp. 144-45. Soustelle speaks of
attacks made by nomadic Indians on others living in settled villages in the Sierra
Gorda at various times from 1691 to 1748: "The chronicles of the time talk of
Indians who had learned to ride horseback and, like the redskins farther north,
attacked the mule trains that tried to trudge across the Sierra. Some of the attackers
even scalped their victims, but in a curiously different way: instead of taking the
scalp, they took the beard and the skin of the chin!"
3. *Land to the West* , Chapters Eight and Nine.
4. Pre-Columbian Terracottas, p. 187. Von Wuthenau's reference here to Egypt is a
reminder that during part of the period of Olmec ascendancy Egypt was ruled by
the 25th or "Ethiopian" Dynasty (712-663 B.C.).
5. Heine-Geldern and Ekholm in a paper included in *Selected Papers of the XXIXth
International Congress of Americanists* (1951) illustrate a "demonic lion" motif of
the Gupta period of Indian history (ninth to eleventh centuries A.D.) as another
instance of parallelism. I myself have found a striking resemblance between a
figurine found in the Totonac archaeological area of Mexico and a "demonic
lion" at Konarak, in the state of Orissa, India.
6. The tradition of the Nestorian Christian foundations in Ceylon and India cannot
satisfactorily be traced to an earlier date than the seventh or eigth centuries A.D.

Chapter Ten – Toys and Arches

1. *The Paths of Culture* pp. 56-7.

Chapter Eleven — Coins and Inscriptions

1. For the material here discussed I am grateful to Dr. Gordon for information he made available to me, and for his provocative book, *Before Columbus.*
2. "He saith unto them, How many loaves have ye? Go and see. And when they knew, they say, Five, and two fishes." Mark 6:38 (Authorized Version). It should be noted here that one of the commonest Christian symbols found in the catacombs at Rome involves various graphic representations of two fish.
3. *Writing*, p. 110.

PART III — THE CULTURAL EVIDENCE

Chapter Twelve — The Monotheistic Tradition

1. Laurette Séjourné, a French archaeologist living and working in Mexico, "believes that Quetzalcoatl was a king living about the time of Christ," according to Irene Nicholson, *Mexican and Central American Mythology*, p. 79.
2. *Ancient, Medieval and Modern Christianity*, p. 3-4.
3. Laurette Séjourné, *Burning Water*, p. 7.
4. This is my own theory. I also believe that the long-nosed Chacs, or rain-gods that are so prominent a feature of the decoration on Mayan temples, represent a further degeneration of the hero's identifying beard.
5. "It is amazing, but now undeniable, that the vocabulary of symbol is to such an extent constant through the world that it must be recognized to represent a single pictorial script, through which realizations of a *tremendum* experienced through life are given statement. Apparent also is the fact that not only in higher cultures, but also among many of the priests and visionaries of the folk cultures, these symbols – or, as we so often say, 'gods' – are not thought to be powers in themselves but are signs through which the powers of life and its revelations are recognized and released: powers of the soul as well as of the living world." (*The Masks of God: Occidental Mythology*, p. 312.)
6. *Ancient, Medieval and Modern Christianity*, p. 150.
7. Walter Krickeberg, Hermann Trimborn, Werner Müller and Otto Zerries, *Pre-Columbian American Religions* (London: Weidenfeld and Nicholson: 1968), pp. 42-3. Krickeberg here quotes Konrad Theodor Preuss, *Religion und Mythologie der Uitoto*, Volumes I and II (Göttingen: 1921, 1923), and Josef Haeken, *Höchgott und Götter im alten Mexico*, Kairos 3 (Salzburg: 1959).
8. The First Epistle General of St. John, 1:1 (Authorized Version.)

Chapter Thirteen — Singers of Songs

1. *Burning Water*, pp. 53-4.
2. O ye sun and moon, bless ye the Lord; praise and exalt him above all for ever.
   O ye stars of heaven, bless ye the Lord; praise and exalt him above all for ever. (The Song of the Three Holy Children: The Apocrypha, 40-41.)

3. Alice Cunningham Fletcher, "The Omaha Tribe," 27th *Annual Report* , Bureau of American Ethnology, Washington, D.C., 1911. Quoted in A. Grove Day, *The Sky Clears* , pp. 104.
4. Hartley Burr Alexander, *The Mythology of All Races* (Boston: 1920). Quoted in A. Grove Day, *The Sky Clears* , p. 165.
5. D.G. Brinton, "Ancient Nahuatl Poetry," *Library of American Aboriginal Literature* , Vol. 7 (Philadelphia: 1887). Quoted in A. Grove Day, *The Sky Clears* , pp. 180-2.
6. Ecclesiastes 11:8. (Authorized Version.)
7. Ecclesiastes 3:20.

Chapter Fourteen — Art and the Soul
1. Frank Whitford, *Kandinsky* , p. 9.
2. At the Rancho la Puerta, near Tecate, Baja California, I have seen great natural boulders on the hillsides which, to an active imagination, readily assume anthropomorphic forms. One group of four huge hooded shapes kneels in an attitude of prayer facing a flat stone resembling an altar. One glance at such wind- and water-weathered natural sculptures and one senses the source of inspiration for much of the monumental art of the pre-Columbian Mexicans.
3. Westheim, *The Art of Ancient Mexico* , pp. 51 and 44.
4. *Ibid.* , pp. 242-3.

PART IV — WAYS AND MEANS

Chapter Fifteen — Vessels and Destinations
1. Acts of the Apostles, Chapter 27.
2. Geoffrey Ashe (in *Land to the West* , pp. 176-83) quotes extensively from Plutarch's account to show that the ancient writer was in possession of astonishingly accurate information about the North Atlantic, locating what may have been the Gulf of the St. Lawrence to within a degree of its correct latitude.

PART V — WHO WAS QUETZALCOATL?

Chapter Sixteen — The New World Hero
1. This is not to imply that the Jewish Christians did not proselytize. They did so most vigorously, but always insisted that Gentile initiates be circumcised first. In other words, they had to become Jews before becoming Christians.

Chapter Seventeen — The Old World Refugee
1. Eusebius, *The Ecclesiastical History* , II, 23.
2. The General Epistle of James, 1:9-11. (Authorized Version.)
3. Luke 6:20. (Authorized Version.)

4. Matthew 5:3. (Authorized Version.)

5. Eusebius, *The Ecclesiastical History*, II, 23.

6. Acts of the Apostles 11:26: "And the disciples were called Christians first in Antioch." (Authorized Version.)

7. Eusebius, *The Ecclesiastical History*, III, 20:1-9.

8. *Jewish Christianity*. In this chapter I have chosen to accept Schoeps' findings which are disputed by many orthodox Christian scholars. For example, Jean Danielou, S.J. in *The Dead Sea Scrolls and Primitive Christianity* (pp. 122-4) professes to trace the origin and development of the faith of the Pella community to an encounter with Christianized Essenes from the monastery at Qumran, destroyed by the Romans in 70 A.D. This speculation seems to me to be unsupported by the evidence accumulated by Schoeps. Hans Conzelmann (in *History of Primitive Christianity*, pp. 134-8) supports Schoeps, as do S.G.F. Brandon and others. It is doubtful whether these conflicting views will ever be resolved. The principal difficulty is the paucity of documentary material. Much evidence was deliberately destroyed. Dr. Hugh J. Schonfield (in *Those Incredible Christians*, p. 124) cites instances of book-burnings by imperial edict: "By the edict of the Emperor Diocletian (A.D. 303) among other instructions, the destruction of Christian sacred books was ordered. When Christianity became the official religion of the Empire, the Christian emperors Theodosius and Valentinian similarly ordered the burning of all writings hostile to Christianity, which included all books deemed heretical." One is inevitably reminded of Bishop Diego de Landa's *auto-da-fé* of the Mayan libraries in 1562. To be fair, one must also cite the action of the Aztec Emperor Itzcoatl who, in the fifteenth century, ordered large numbers of manuscripts burned because, according to Jacques Soustelle (in *Mexico*, p. 29) "they gave an inaccurate account of the history of Mexico City." It would appear that once books appear in civilized societies, book-burnings inevitably follow.

9. "Verily I say unto you, that this generation shall not pass, till all these things be done." Mark 13:30. (Authorized Version.)

10. 11:19. (New English Bible.)

11. Isaiah 23:12. (New English Bible.)

PART VI — CONCLUSIONS

Chapter Eighteen — The Man of Izamal

1. It is interesting to compare their reception with that accorded the Norse colonists on Newfoundland nearly nine centuries later. There, Norse belligerence was met by native belligerence; and since the Norse were no better armed than their "Skraeling" opponents, they were eventually driven from their settlements.

2. Geoffrey Ashe (ed.), *The Quest for America*, p. 131.

3. "So these two (Barnabas and Saul), sent out on their mission by the Holy Spirit, came down to Seleucia and from there sailed to Cyprus. Arriving at Salamis, they

declared the word of God in the Jewish synagogues. They had John with them as their assistant. They went through the whole island as far as Paphos . . . . Leaving Paphos, Paul and his companions went by sea to Perga in Pamphylia." Acts of the Apostles 13:3-5, 13. (New English Bible.)

4. Sunday = sun day; Monday = moon day; Tuesday = Tiw's day; Wednesday = Woden's day; Thursday = Thor's day; Friday = Frig's day. All these are from Scandinavian and Germanic sources. Saturday is Saturn's day, from Roman mythology.

5. Pope Gregory the Great to the Abbot Mellitus on the departure of the Abbot for England. Quoted in Brian Branston, *The Lost Gods of England* (London: 1957), p. 45.

6. The missionary aspect of the Quetzalcoatl cult is one of its most fascinating and persistent features. Down to the Spanish conquest the mysterious guild of the *pochtecas* continued to carry out the work of their founder. The *pochtecas* were merchant-missionaries, practising a strict code of ethics under the aegis of the Quetzalcoatl cult, conveying ideas as well as goods, preaching their protector's kingdom – which was not of this world. Irene Nicholson (in *Mexican and Central American Mythology*, pp. 92-93) says: "The *pochtecas* never made a show of their riches or power, but always behaved humbly . . . . They were mysterious people in the ancient world, exercising their influence silently, behind the scenes, but acting as a thread binding the whole pattern of Nahua-Maya culture together and using coastal towns as centres from which to radiate their varied influences." It was undoubtedly this guild of proselytizing merchants, operating from Teotihuacán ("the place where one became a god"), a city without fortifications, where no offensive weapons nor traces of warlike activity have ever been found, that was responsible for the extension of the influence of Teotihuacán throughout the entire Middle American area, from the Valley of Mexico to the Isthmus of Panama. It was probably a canoe-load of *pochtecas* that Christopher Columbus met near the island of Guanaja, off the coast of Honduras in 1502, on his closest approach to the mainland of the Americas, which he is credited (erroneously) with discovering. It is more than likely that this guild was responsible for the survival of the cult and teachings of Quetzalcoatl through the great social and political upheavals that rent the fabric of the civilizations of pre-Columbian America at least three times during the Christian era.

Bibliography

The following is a partial list of the sources consulted in the preparation of this book. A complete listing of the more than 2,000 printed works I have consulted in forty years of reading in this field would bore the general reader and inordinately lengthen what was intended from the first to be a slim volume.

Allen, F.A.	*Polynesian Antiquities.* Copenhagen: 1884.
Andrews, E. Wyllys	"Dzibilchaltún: Lost City of the Maya," *National Geographic Magazine*, January 1959.
Ashe, Geoffrey	*Land to the West.* London: Collins, 1962.
(ed.)	*The Quest for America.* London: Praeger Publishers, 1971.
Bernal, Ignacio	*Mexico Before Cortés: Art, History and Legend.* Translated by Willis Branstone. New York: Dolphin Books, 1963.
	Mexican Wall Paintings. New York. Mentor-Unesco Art Books, 1965.
Blom, Frans	*The Conquest of Yucatan.* Boston: Houghton Mifflin, 1936.
Brennan, Louis A.	*American Dawn.* New York: The Macmillan Company, 1970.
	No Stone Unturned. New York: Random House, 1959.
Brinton, Daniel G.	*American Hero-Myths.* Philadelphia: H.C. Watts and Company, 1882.
	The Annals of the Cakchiquels. Philadelphia: Library of Aboriginal American Literature, No. VI, 1885.
	The Maya Chronicle. Philadelphia: Library of Aboriginal American Literature, No. I, 1882.
Burland, Cottie A.	*The Gods of Mexico.* London: Eyre & Spottiswood, 1967.

	The People of the Ancient Americas. London: Hamlyn House, 1970.
Bushnell, G.H.S.	*Ancient Arts of the Americas.* London: Thames and Hudson, 1965.
Bowditch, Charles P.	*The Temples of the Cross, the Foliated Cross and the Sun at Palenque.* Cambridge, Mass.: The Peabody Museum, 1906.
(ed.)	*Mexican and Central American Antiquities, Calendar Systems and History.* Twenty-four papers by Eduard Seler, E. Förstemann, Paul Schellhas, Carl Sapper, and E.P. Dieseldorff. Translated from the German under the supervision of Charles P. Bowditch. Washington, D.C.: Bulletin 28, Bureau of American Ethnology, 1904.
Campbell, Joseph	*The Masks of God: Primitive Mythology.* New York: Viking Press, 1959.
	The Masks of God: Oriental Mythology. New York: Viking Press, 1962.
	The Masks of God: Occidental Mythology. New York: Viking Press, 1964.
Carrillo y Ancona, Crescencio	*Historia Antigua de Yucatan.* Merida, Yucatan, Mexico: Compañia Tipográfica Yucateca, S.A., 1937.
Ceram, C.W.	*The First American.* New York: Harcourt Brace Jovanovich, 1971.
Charnay, Désiré	*The Ancient Cities of the New World.* New York: Harper and Brothers, 1887.
Churchward, James	*The Lost Continent of Mu.* New York: Ives Washburn, Inc., 1932.
Coe, Michael D.	*America's First Civilization.* Toronto: McClelland and Stewart, 1968.
	The Maya. London: Thames and Hudson, 1966.
Chapin, Henry and Smith, F.G. Walton	*The Ocean River.* New York: Scribners, 1952.
Cohane, John Philip	*The Key.* New York: Crown Publishers, 1969.
Collis, Maurice	*Cortés and Montezuma.* London: Faber & Faber, Ltd., 1954.
Coulborn, Rushton	*The Origin of Civilized Societies.* Princeton, N.J.: Princeton University Press, 1959.
Covarrubias, Miguel	*Mexico South: The Isthmus of Tehuantepec.* New York: Alfred A. Knopf, Inc., 1946.

	Indian Art of Mexico and Central America. New York: Alfred A. Knopf, Inc., 1957.
Craveri, Marcello	*The Life of Jesus*. Translated by Charles Lam Markmann. New York: Grove Press, 1967.
Day, A. Grove	*The Sky Clears: Poetry of the American Indians*. Lincoln, Nebraska: University of Nebraska Press, 1951.
Diaz del Castillo, Bernal	*The Discovery and Conquest of Mexico*. Edited by Genaro García. Translated by A.P. Maudslay. New York: Farrar, Straus and Cudahy, 1956.
Dimont, Max I.	*Jews, God and History*. Toronto: Signet Books, 1966.
Diringer, David	*Writing*. London: Thames and Hudson, 1962.
Donnelly, Ignatius	*Atlantis, the Antediluvian World*. New York: Harper and Brothers, 1882.
Duff, Wilson	*Images Stone B.C.; Thirty Centuries of Northwest Coast Indian Sculpture*. Toronto: Oxford University Press, 1975.
Ekholm, Gordon F.	"Is American Indian Culture Asiatic?," *Natural History Magazine* , October 1950. "Wheeled Toys in Mexico," *American Antiquity* , Vol. 2, No. 4, 1946.
Ekholm, Gordon F. and	"Significant Parallels in the Symbolic Arts of Southern
Heine-Geldern, Robert	Asia and Middle America," *Proceedings of the 29th International Congress of Americanists* , Vol. 1. Chicago: University of Chicago Press, 1951.
Erosa Peniche, José A.	*Guide to the Ruins of Chichén-Itzá*. Translated from the Spanish by John W. Germon. Merida, Yucatan, Mexico: Editorial Yikal Maya Than, 1947.
	Guide Book to the Ruins of Uxmal. Translated from the Spanish by Julio Granados. Merida, Yucatan, Mexico: Editorial Yikal Maya Than, 1948.
Eusebius	*The Essential Eusebius*. Selected and translated by Colm Luibheid. Toronto: Mentor-Omega Books, 1966.
Fiske, John	*The Discovery of America*. Boston: Houghton Mifflin, 1902.
Gallenkamp, Charles	*Maya*. New York: Pyramid Publications, 1962.
Gann, T.W.F.	*Ancient Cities and Modern Tribes*. New York: Charles Scribner's Sons, 1926.

	The Maya Indians of Southern Yucatan and Northern British Honduras. Bulletin No. 64. Washington: Bureau of American Ethnology, 1918.
Gann, Thomas and Thompson, J. Eric	*The History of the Maya*. New York: Charles Scribner's Sons, 1931.
Gladwin, Harold S.	*Men Out of Asia*. New York: McGraw-Hill Book Co., Inc., 1947.
Goodwin, William B.	*The Ruins of Great Ireland in New England*. Boston: Meador, 1946.
Gordon, Cyrus H.	*Before Columbus*. New York: Crown Publishers, Inc., 1971.
Guide Books	The following are all published by the Institute Nacional de Antropologia e Historia of Mexico: *Copilco-Cuicuilco* (Unsigned). *Mayan Hall*. By Roman Piña Chan. *Maya Cities*. By Roman Piña Chan. *Morelos*. By Eduardo Noguera. *The Tabasco Museums*. By Carlos Pellicer. *Teotihuacán*. By Jorge R. Acosta. *Tulum*. (Unsigned). *Uxmal*. By Alberto Ruz Lhuillier.
Guignebert, Charles	*Jesus*. Translated from the French by S.H. Hooke. New York: University Books, 1956. *The Christ*. Translated from the French by Peter Ouzts and Phyllis Cooperman. New York: University Books, 1968. *Ancient, Medieval and Modern Christianity*. First English translation 1927. Reprint New York: University Books, 1961.
Heine-Geldern, Robert	*The Civilization of Ancient America*. (*The Origin of Ancient Civilizations*, Vol I. Selected Papers of the XXIXth International Congress of Americanists.) Chicago: University of Chicago Press, 1951.
Herrera, Antonio de	*Historia General de las Indias Occidentalis*. Madrid: 1601.
Herrmann, Paul	*Conquest by Man*. Translated from the German by Michael Bullock. New York: Harper and Brothers, 1954.

	The Great Age of Discovery. Translated from the German by Arnold J. Pomerans. New York: Harper and Brothers, 1958.
Heyerdahl, Thor	*American Indians in the Pacific.* London, Oslo and Stockholm: George Allen and Unwin, 1952.
Hibben, Frank C.	*The Lost Americans.* New York: Thomas Y. Crowell Company, 1947.
Hyams, Edward and Ordish, George	*The Last of the Incas.* New York: Simon & Schuster, 1963.
Irwin, Constance	*Fair Gods and Stone Faces.* New York: St. Martin's Press, 1963.
Kenny, James F.	*The Legend of St. Brendan.* Royal Society of Canada. Series 3, Vol. 14 (1920).
Landa, Fr. Diego de	*Relacion de las Cosas de Yucatan.* First Yucatecan edition. Merida, Yucatan, Mexico: E.G. Triay e Hijos, 1938.
Le Plongeon, Augustus	*Queen Moo and the Egyptian Sphinx.* New York: Published by the author, 1900.
Leicht, Hermann	*Pre-Inca Art and Culture.* New York: Orion Press, 1960.
Lorang, Sister Mary Corde	*Footloose Scientists in Mayan America.* New York: Charles Scribner's Sons, 1966.
Macgowan, Kenneth	*Early Man in the New World.* New York: Macmillan, 1950.
Makemson, Maud Worcester (ed.)	*The Book of the Jaguar Priest.* A translation of the Book of Chilam Balam of Tizimin. New York: Henry Schuman, 1951.
Marett, Sir Robert	*Archaeological Tours from Mexico City.* Mexico City: Ediciones Tolteca, S.A., 1964.
Mason, Gregory	*Silver Cities of Yucatan.* New York: G.P. Putnam's Sons, 1927.
	Columbus Came Late. New York: Century, 1931.
	South of Yesterday. New York: Henry Holt & Co., Inc., 1940.
Mason, J. Alden	*The Ancient Civilizations of Peru.* Harmondsworth, Middlesex, England: Penguin Books, 1957.
McKern, W.C.	"An Hypothesis for the Asiatic Origin of the Woodland Culture," *American Antiquity* , Vol. 3, pp. 138-143, 1937.

Mead, G.R.S.   *Fragments of a Faith Forgotten.* New York: University Books, n.d.

Means, Philip Ainsworth   *Ancient Civilizations of the Andes.* New York: Charles Scribner's Sons, 1931.

History of the Spanish Conquest of Yucatan and of the Itzas. Cambridge, Mass.: Papers of the Peabody Museum of American Archaeology and Ethnology, Vol. 7, 1917.

Fall of the Inca Empire and the Spanish Rule in Peru: 1530-1780. New York: Charles Scribner's Sons, 1932.

Mitchell, J. Leslie   *The Conquest of the Maya.* London: Jarrolds, 1934.

Moorhouse, A.C.   *The Triumph of the Alphabet.* New York: Henry Schuman, 1953.

Morison, Samuel Eliot   *The European Discovery of America; the Northern Voyages, A.D. 500-1600.* London: Oxford University Press, 1971.

Morley, Sylvanus G.   *The Ancient Maya.* Revised by G.W. Brainerd. Stanford: Stanford University Press, 1968.

Morley, Sylvanus G. and   "The Maya Chronicles," *Contributions to American*
Vasquez, Alfredo Brarrera   *Anthropology and History* , Vol. X, No. 48. Washington, D.C.; Carnegie Institution, 1949.

Morris, Earl H.   *The Temple of the Warriors.* New York: Charles Scribner's Sons, 1931.

Nicholson, Irene   *Mexican and Central American Mythology.* London: Paul Hamlyn, 1967.

Peissel, Michel   *The Lost World of Quintana Roo.* New York: E.P. Dutton & Co., Inc., 1963.

Pendergast, David M. (ed.) *Palenque: The Walker-Caddy Expedition to the Ancient Maya City, 1839-1840.* Norman, Oklahoma: The University of Oklahoma Press, 1970.

Peterson, Frederick A.   *Ancient Mexico.* New York: G.P. Putnam's Sons, 1959.

Posnansky, Arthur   *Tihuanacu, the Cradle of American Man.* New York: J.J. Augustin, 1945.

Prescott, William H.   *History of the Conquest of Mexico.* New York: Bantam Books, 1964.

History of the Conquest of Peru. New York: Modern Library, 1936.

Rodman, Selden   *Mexican Journal*. New York: Devin-Adair Co., 1958.

Roys, Ralph L.   *The Book of Chilam Balam of Chumayel*. Norman, Oklahoma: University of Oklahoma Press, 1967.

Roys, Lawrence   "The Engineering Knowledge of the Maya," *Contributions to American Archaeology*, No. 6. Washington, D.C.: Carnegie Institution, 1934.

Sahagún, Fr. Bernardino de   *Historia General de las Cosas de Nueva España*. Mexico City: Editorial Nueva España, S.A., 1946.

Schoeps, Hans-Joachim   *Jewish Christianity*. Translated by Douglas R.A. Hare. Philadelphia: Fortress Press, 1969. (*Das Judenchristentum*. Berne, Switzerland: 1964).

Sejourné, Laurette   *Burning Water*. New York: Grove Press, 1960.

Silverberg, Robert   *Mound Builders of Ancient America*. Greenwich, Conn.: New York Graphic Society, 1968.

Soustelle, Jacques   *Mexico*. (Archaeologia Mundi Series). New York: World Publishing Co., 1967.

                                             Daily Life of the Aztecs. Translated by Patrick O'Brian. London: Pelican Books, 1968.

                                           The Four Suns. New York: Grossman Publishers, 1971.

Spence, Lewis   *The Gods of Mexico*. New York: Frederick A. Stokes Company, 1923.

Spinden, Herbert Joseph   *Maya Art and Civilization*. Indian Hills, Colorado: The Falcon's Wing Press, 1957.

Stephens, John L.   *Incidents of Travel in Central America, Chiapas, and Yucatan*. New York: Harper and Brothers, 1841.

Thompson, Edward Herbert   *People of the Serpent*. New York: Capricorn Books, 1965.

Thompson, J. Eric S.   *The Rise and Fall of Maya Civilization*. Norman, Oklahoma: University of Oklahoma Press, 1954.

                                           Maya History and Religion. Norman, Oklahoma: University of Oklahoma Press, 1970.

                                           The Moon Goddess in Middle America with Notes on Related Deities. Washington, D.C.: Carnegie Institution, Publication 509, Contribution 29, 1939.

Vaillant, George C.   *Aztecs of Mexico*. Pelican Books. New York: Doubleday & Company, Inc., 1966.

	"A Bearded Mystery," *Natural History* , Vol. XXXI, No. 3, May-June 1931.
Verrill, A. Hyatt	*Old Civilizations of the New World*. Indianapolis: The Bobbs-Merrill Co., 1929.
Verrill, A. Hyatt and Verrill, Ruth	*America's Ancient Civilizations*. New York: G.P. Putnam's Sons, 1953.
Von Däniken, Erich	*Chariots of the Gods?* Translated by Michael Heron. New York: Bantam Books, 1971.
Von Hagen, Victor W.	*The Aztec: Man and Tribe*. New York: Mentor Books, 1958.
	World of the Maya. New York: Mentor Books, 1960.
Von Wuthenau, Alexander	*Pre-Columbian Terracottas*. Translated by the author and Irene Nicholson. London: Methuen, 1970.
	Unexpected Faces in Ancient America: 1500 B.C. – A.D. 1500. New York: Crown Publishers Inc., 1975.
Von Winning, Hasso	*Pre-Columbian Art*. London: Thames & Hudson, 1969.
Waldeck, J.F. de	*Voyage pittoresque et archéologique dans la province d'Yucatan*. Paris: Dufor et Cie., 1838.
Wauchope, Robert	*Lost Tribes and Sunken Continents*. Chicago: University of Chicago Press, 1962.
Westheim, Paul	*The Sculpture of Ancient Mexico*. Translated from the Spanish into English by Ursula Bernard. Translated into Spanish from the original German by Mariana Frank. New York: Anchor Books, 1963.
	The Art of Ancient Mexico. Translated by Ursula Bernard. New York: Anchor Books, 1965.
Whitford, Frank	*Kandinsky*. London: Paul Hamlyn, 1967.
Willard, T.A.	*The City of the Sacred Well*. New York: Century Co., 1926.
Wormington, H.M.	*Ancient Man in North America*. Denver, Colorado: The Denver Museum of Natural History, 1957.